Reviews for Breathtaking:

Elizabeth shares a journey which indeed belongs to each of us. Passing through moments of deep joy, loss or longing, she discovers the shining connection to all being and shares her insights freely. This book will take it's place among the recorded experiences of spiritual seekers - a talisman for us to carry close.

Lark Leonard, Earth keeper

Elizabeth's life fully lived has created a book fully alive - alive with the breath of wisdom, the energy of joy in mystery, a dance through all we create and are created by. Come for a dip or immerse yourself fully, find your own truth in her words and images. find myself smiling and nodding through these pages; the rest of my day is brighter and fuller for her gift of sharing. Don't miss the fun!"

Eric Read. Raja Yoga Teacher

Elizabeth Bunker's Breathtaking is a deep dive into the science-based, practical and spiritual dimensions of the breath. Drawing on her experience as a long-time yoga teacher and student of life, she lays out a practice for delving into the breath's power and using that power to live a more conscious life. Both manual and spiritual memoir, Ms. Bunker invites us to explore what it means to be both human and awake.

Mara Bright, author of The Constant Heart, Writing Coach

Elizabeth has written a beautiful book in several different ways. In the first part - her Memoire - her style is creative and flowing with both passion and humor that can bring you to hysterical laughter and grips you with her story.

The remainder of the book is more instructional. Elizabeth is a masterful teacher of Yoga and therefore the breath, and here she guides us simply and directly with these 11 Breaths to attain something profound for our own lives. We only have to practice! She makes this seem an effortless effort, with immediate results.

I find Breath #2 particularly important to steady the heart, especially since there is so much electricity and ELFs bombarding us these days that can throw our hearts off balance lickety split. I'm looking forward to using this book to enhance my healing practice - for myself and others. Thank you Elizabeth. This is a work of Art.

Heather Joyce Wolfe, RN, BCPP *Author of A Guide to Breast Cancer:A Whole Body Guide to Prevention and Healing - Conventional and Alternative.*

The stories from her life; that's what drew me in. The stunningly beautiful prose that borders on lyric poetry. I couldn't help it. I kept skipping around to the memoirs wanting to read yet another moving, wry, funny, memoir told in her supremely refreshing unconventional style. You've not read a writer like this.

David Zucker; author of Poetry in Motion, MythMasters, The Shakespeare Guyz, and Uncle Carmello

BREATHTAKING

Growing up Mystic in America

Breathing,
the alchemy of
embracing our fear,
allowing what is
and
remembering our True Self
&
Eleven breaths for vitality, peace and life

Elizabeth Bunker

The dazzling and heart opening
Eleven star journey into the mysteries of
the Breath

You will live the way you breathe.

Whoever knows their Self, knows the Lord.[1]

For David
Anam Cara in Truth,
Love and Play

Invitation

Breath is Life

We too must make ourselves empty, that the great Soul of the universe may fill us with its breath.[2]

Innocence: The wonder of wonder

If you had asked the child, what was the theme of her nights, she would invite you, as I do now, to come and get on your knees. That's it. Come into the room with the tiny bed and the radio and now place your elbows on the sill of this window. Yes, flick away the dead moth, the ladybug, the flies and set your gaze wide. It is out there, do you see? Look through the darkness and close one eye and soon they will appear. The winged ones first. We can make them disappear together, but for now, let them appear. Miss Gail's magnolia trees are no longer. Are they still there? Who knows, as the night takes with it all forms, all that seems so dense and certain in the day.

Now, look up, look into that indigo blue with its net of lights. What looks like a traveling star may be Apollo in his chariot or a space ship; or the Four Horsemen of the Apocalypse blown off course.

Or maybe not. Listen, you know yourself that nothing is as it seems. This is indisputable. Don't be hornswaggled. That jot of brightness above the trees? It isn't a star at all, it's an orb or a satellite or maybe a fire beetle; those flashes of light we collect and put into jars to light our way in the forest. One moment it all seems perfectly clear and the next it burbles and turns into something else. It all rolls on fluid and vague as images, thoughts, beliefs, memories, fears come and then, as the sun, they disappear.

Mystery coming out of mystery.

Now close your eyes; listen up. Breathe in. There are the night sounds, the thrumming sounds may be the cicadas. That ruffling shir of wing may be the robin's; the chicka-clack is surely the raccoon moving down the oak tree. Or not. Beyond this first circle of sounds, riding out on our curiosity, is that hum that comes from the night sky. Do you hear the waves of sound? Something is breathing as the wind slides over the face. Something wonderful is happening here.

Something breathtaking.

Her window opens, as yours does, to what seems an infinite and unstoppable sky dotted with a moving show of stars, planets, space ships, visitors and visions. It is a wonderment that no one talks about it in the family. She wants to know, "What keeps them shining? What are they floating in? In what are we floating? What holds us and keeps us from crashing into each other?" The Big Mother is silent. Secrets were locked in her purse, her eyes and her lingerie drawer.

Just as you have wondered.

When the shooting stars appear or an eclipse of the moon, they, the Big mother and Big Father, the sister and dog join together in watching. Awe and no talk prevailed. Except for those times in the sky, nobody talks about it. The child comes here, to her secret place every night. No mystery story can bring the waters of the child's heart into such a wondrous state as does this night sky. Sometimes the hands shake as she leans on elbows and looks out. Sometimes the breath stops, for it is here that secrets hide.

When the grandfather dies in a car accident they say he has come here, to the sky. When the dog, Cinders, is hit by a car they say she has come here to rest in Dog Heaven. The beautiful horse Goldie is here and no one speaks his name.

So much hides in the rafters of this house, so much goes unspoken here that wanting to know the secrets is a mission. She made it a quest and an exploration without leaving the sill, to uncover the secrets at the heart of this strange and magical place. For this celestial earth wherein hangs all manner of floating things along with moons, stars, comets, flying squirrels, atoms, crows, her mother's smile, her grandfather's pipe and who knows what else? What if this becomes a purpose, a way of life, to ask, to wonder, to wander and learn about the secrets?

These questions live and grow as the child grows and as she leaves behind this window only to find another and then another as the father moves them from town to town. These questions seem, all of them, to fall from this wanton and serene wonder, the night sky. To enter the world of her father she must remain quiet and behave as one who is not here. Invisible. To enter the inchoate night secrets she must follow the unspoken word, the one still vague word that is taking on a silhouette within, urging her on: escape.

Escape. To leave the house whenever possible.

From the clothes which bind.

From the house which can twist the belly into knots.

From the teachers and their judgments that cut

From the body which can hurt and still presses in so tightly.

From this house of happiness and sudden rage squalls.

From this world with it's excitements and bellyaches.

From this place of hard knocks and spider web miracles.

For what is it that gives birth to escape? It is the other

feeling, the other knowing word.

Home.

That which she knows above all else in a sudden flare
which burns through all confusion; this is not her real home. It is
a place in which to watch and listen, to dance alone and sing
when the house is empty. A place in which to be vigilant.

Along the way

Growing up I believed that at some point when I had
created something rare, written a poem or a song, made a film,
painted rainbows on oil tanks with Sister Corita, jumped a horse
over a five foot fence, or done something really smashing, then,
like winning the Noble Prize, I would be shown the secrets of the
universe. Until then? I wasn't worthy. Life was struggle and failure
and so be it; so my father warned me. So to claim the treasure
map that leads to that prestigious place hinted at in all great
stories, there must be fires to put out, prairies to map. So I waited.
It would take effort to attain this grand work.

Just as you have waited and struggled.

Beneath the sense of isolation, the moments of confusion
and laughter, the dreams and thoughts and the plethora of forms
arising and disappearing, there was something waiting to be
allowed. This deep feeling kept me alert. Within life's infinite
circus of mirrors there were strange glimpses and visions and

dreams and it all felt like a great show whose meaning was part of a club. I looked to the fathers. I looked to the philosophers and theologians in college. Mostly, I looked to the artists. I even looked to the hunger artists. I looked to the musicians. Then I noticed that most were otherwise involved; no one was looking back. No one talked of the night, or the dragonflies or the star world. Or of this thing called 'death' or 'heaven.' Nobody I knew really asked about it. I waited.

Coming into Presence

What we all share is experience. This book comes out of experience. Yet, remember here, immediate experience cannot be replicated. Words are already three steps away. Words come after the revelation, the feelings and perceptions and after the mind seeks to find an expression. Finally, the mind wants to name it, label it. Then those words, in the form of ink-spots, are put on the medium of this paper you are holding. Or the kindle screen. It all begins with an empty blank page. A field on which words can appear. I sit, like Alice in Wonderland, before she is distracted by the world, allowing the silence to speak. She may return to the peace of the blank page. That came for me years after I had begun the drama of seeking. Answering a call from within.

In essence this book is simply a request that you regard your own life as a sacred enterprise, as a quest to claim what is hidden. To know your natural and True Self takes a certain courage. At first? It may take a leap of faith. I invite you to see your life filled with signposts, guides, masters who want to share with you the only purpose life has. Yet, for me, it was and is my ongoing wish to share the ups and downs, the mystic realizations, the constant remembrance and attuning with indwelling spirit. And yes, the terrible loneliness, the failures, and the unbounded cry, "Hey! Speak Spirit. I am hanging onto this ledge. With one finger." Life lived now from breath to breath is a surprise, always.

In truth, the breath helps bring you smack dab into Presence. Some speak of it as ordinary knowing or as the Universal Presence. Some might call it the Now. There are, oh, many words for Cosmic consciousness, Christ consciousness, God consciousness, Nirvana, fulfillment, Enlightenment. Yes, it has many names. As you dip beneath the persona mind, dive within, feel it as an exploration of this shimmering presence. It is the most exciting, illuminating, heart rending and misunderstood of all of this life. It is living at a higher existence. For, in truth, it comes before all experience. Finally? It will bring you into freedom, which is our legacy, our home.

As it is true, that "all the way to heaven is heaven,"[1] so it is true here. For the very experience of the breath, of allowing it to open doors within, of the exquisite flow and afterwards the stillness, revitalizes all systems of your being. It carries wisdom. Yes. So I am glad you like surprises. But do not take my word for it, no, please, experiment. Be willing. Be open. It is also about paying attention to something we usually ignore; something we take for granted. Like a fish swimming around asking, "Where is this thing you call water? Its a danged lie. I don't believe it cuz I have never seen it."

Becoming aware of the breath you may delight in more fruitful modes of being; caterpillar to butterfly. Do you see? As you breathe with attention, something emerges; something unexpected. There is no end to the depth of the infinite; no end to this we call the body.

Revelation

We live each moment in the presence of revelation; the revealing of what has been hidden. Revelation is, that is all. Nothing that is not here, right now, is available somewhere or sometime down the line. The question always is, where am I? Who am I?

If this were a "How to" book, I would not include the stories of a life. Yet, it is more of a "What if?" book. For growing up life seemed a tight, claustrophobic and empty enterprise without meaning. It was a world without a compass. This was way before I fell into a realization and a meaning beyond my imagination. Then, nothing was ordinary and everything unexpected.

What if, what we learn in school and from the culture has nothing to do with our True Nature? Much of it I had to unlearn to know Reality. What if, we arrive whole and perfect, innocent and alert but then? We forgot our way. Now we are remembering. What if, our True Nature is revealing that we have all the powers of heaven and earth, but are only now choosing to use them? That Heaven is right now and right here? What if, you are part of this awakening which is remembering?

You will see the word "ponder" often in this book and "make your home in the breath." It is a call to drop into a state of receptivity. Take three deep breaths, allow the energy to fall into the low belly with each one. Be empty. This is your life. Use time wisely.

The deep breath is a magic that you give to yourself. It holds the Holy Spirit of your being, and embraces the wisdom, light and guidance you need to melt into your True Self. It offers possibility for expansion. It offers opportunity for peace. It offers opportunity for a new angle of vision.

If you simply notice the breath throughout the day you are taking the energy away from the chattering persona mind. Away from the limitations of thoughts. This leads to deepening the sense of consciousness. Breath is not usually, in your daily routine life, something you do; it is something you notice. If you bring your attention to the breath for an hour each day, the rewards will be noticed.

The eleven breaths here are called "pranayam" or mastery of the life force. It involves "effortless effort." The fruits of the breath come after it is over.

Notice that what you desire you manifest. I have found that all desires are, finally, the desire to return home to our original Essential Nature. For here alone is freedom, truth, love and fulfillment.

Preface

Breath is life. We all know this. We take it for granted. But most of us do not truly reflect on it or take full advantage of this basic alchemy.

Breath is an alchemy. Every cell of our being is waiting for this elixir we call breath. The cells are the building blocks of our body. This means that all organs, tissues, bones, blood, everything, depend upon this breath. Rhythmic breathing with attention fills the blood with pure light energy and oxygen, ignites the heart in its work, stimulates the brain and affects the digestive and elimination systems as well. Real health follows those who breathe with attention and gratitude.

More than this, it brings you to the heart. Breath is a spiritual way that brought me out of the head and into the heart.

*

Let yourself fall to the ground

Truth is universal. What is it most of us humans desire? Is it not happiness? Is it not peace? Is it not truth? How we go about it is varied and often perplexing. My wonder question is, would the world not be a place of peace and joy if we allow this higher existence? Our true purpose here - the peace of God? The answer we well know. So living from the persona-ego mind has not brought us into that place of "love without conditions" to which Jesus and so many sages, rishis, masters have pointed. Yet, always and ever we are immersed in a field of infinite potential, yes, infinite love. At this moment this Presence, this essence of the Infinite holds you and breathes you as you. The question is, if the Infinite, that which birthed you, is always right here and now, where are you?

A Proposition

Here is my proposition: what if, for this journey, you don't need new clothes, or even a new pen, but you may want to take off your shoes, twirl around a few times, spin in place, fall down and relax into the earth. Or dance. Take a long walk. Hug the dog. Surprise the fish. Walk, do Tai Chi, Yoga or swim in a lake. Then, sit and feel into this body.

Or simply? Take three deep breaths. Anchor them in the belly. All of this takes you out of the persona mind, out of a limited sense of who you are. Then, truly feel into the body which you inhabit. Truly incarnate in this body. The body is not what you think it is; for here all is possible. You are invited to awaken from the dream, that is all.

Breath is always in the Present in this arising. And here, now, is the only place you come into your True Nature. Yes, there is nothing to "get," for you already are THAT. This realization shows us how paradoxical spiritual truth is.

Spirituality is the highest Psychology

The Mystic is willing to explore the Self and thereby the cosmos which is both Infinite and personal. Don't be afraid, don't hold back. Grace comes in the form of many teachers and many ways.

There will be a letting go of old habits and thoughts. While we explore and allow, the breath soothes the nerves and quiets the heart. Here? All is as it is. To see with the eyes of the heart is where breath will take you - if you allow. And this you will experience for yourself. The breath invites you inside, to the kingdom of God, to where your true Self resides. If you fix your eyes only on the things of this world you will be distracted, as I was for so long.

Let go of being serious.

Now, this all may sound very serious, but I assure you that it is not. Not one bit. Only the persona mind is serious; reflect on that. The mystic, that one who knows this life is a complete mystery, lives life as a wonderful gift to be drunk as the purest nectar and enjoyed and lived as a ceaseless dance.

An empty cup allows itself to be filled anew.

Remember once again, what took me some time to discover; the way is not serious. The way is simple. Only a passion for Truth and Reality is absolutely necessary. We are here to play in this Soul school which is this earth plane. We are here to remember. Are you willing? If so, we travel together in this breathing universe. If so? Take my hand. I am holding the hands of so many that we form an infinite web, a fractal jewel that lights up the earth. That lights up the cosmos.

-

- Elizabeth, 2019

Truth is not the laws or in the pages of books, but in
your heart and in your spirit…in your breath, your blood,
your bone; in your flesh, your bowels, your eyes, your ears,
and in every little part of your body.

Everybody knows, in their bones, that something is eternal, and
that something has to do with human beings. … There is
something way down deep that is eternal about every human
being.[3]

Those who have never heard the word 'enlightenment' or 'awakening' are nonetheless vessels in which the Infinite lives as them and through them. For creation cannot be separate from it's creation.

We are living in a world that is
absolutely transparent
and
the Divine is shining through it all the time.
This is not just a nice story or a fable. It is true.[4]

Table of Contents

Preface xiii

WINTER 1

memoir - Masters 2

memoir - On the Bus 25

SPRING 55

memoir - North Stars and Lightning Rods 64

memoir - Chariots 103

memoir - Still on the Bus 114

SUMMER 131

memoir - The Questing Beast 132

Masters and Guides 142

memoir - Masters and Guides 143

memoir - Zen Basketball - David Zucker 152

memoir - In Pursuit of the Tiger 161

memoir - Breathing light 166

FALL 169

memoir - North Stars and Wild Horses 183

memoir - Grace 190

memoir - Forgiveness, letting go of Guilt 198

memoir - The Dance of Anger, the Dance of Love 204

WINTER AGAIN 208

memoir - I first met you Jesus 209

Memoir - Crane Girl 232

memoir - Shimmering Sudsy Bath of Sexy Spirit 240

SPRING AGAIN 249

memoir - The Doorway 255

memoir - Grace again 265

Breath #1 - The Breath of Presence 271

Breath #2 - The Heartbeat Rhythm 275

Breath #3 - The Viloma Breath 277

Breath #4 - The Ujayyi Breath 279

Breath #5 - The Taoist breath 285

Breath #6 - Lovesbreath I and II 293

Breath #7 - The Qigong breath. Heaven & Earth 305

Breath #8 ~ The Kapalabhati Breath................................307
Breath #9 ~ The Lakshmi Breath, the cooling Breath 313
Breath #10 ~ The Tonglen breath of giving and receiving 315
Breath #11 ~ Breathing Nature 317
Websites of interest: 325
Endnotes..326

WINTER

Creation and vision

What happens to the body/mind when you breathe?

It expands. It opens. Each cell opens to accept this fresh lights filled breath; the lungs, the whole chest cavity expands, yes. And the biofield or aura around you expands as well. In this moment you give yourself that opportunity to expand the vision; to be clear here, this breath opens you to a new way of looking at what has appeared to be very constricted. To a new way of 'seeing'. To coming into this Present moment fully and wholly which is holy.

Make your home in the Breath

memoir - Masters

A student of a certain Zen Master told him, "I find that focusing on the breath is boring." The Master grabbed him and pushed him under the pond water for a minute. The student came up thrashing for air. " Now, do you find the breath boring?" The Master inquired. Zen story

My first master was sorrel and white and ready to move at anytime. Skittish, he could smell a cougar forty miles away. He air-scented, flaring those huge nostrils as he ran away from tight spaces and up hills to reach infinite vistas. These ways of his became my ways of being as well. As my grandmother Geneva said so many times,

"You become what you choose to hang out with. Choose your friends with care." She knew and laughed and winked.

My first master and friend was Horse. They called him Bobolink. Every Saturday, when I was nine years old, I rode a bus with thirty other children to a place called Joy Farm held in the cow pastures and cornfields of southern Wisconsin,

Under a Titian blue sky, my teachers stood, expectant. Exhausted wood buildings leaned together all smelling of hay, alfalfa, manure, the must of webs and flies and the nocturnal bats. Here, where the light fell down in spears, my fears lined up rear-end to rear-end. For it was here, as I saddled up, that I held sway over all creation. Once in the saddle? I soared. Immortal, unshakeable, I was the princess of Horsedom. Fear was my greatest happiness. And fear was always with me.

For that summer, as I rode the proud sorrel with a blaze of white running down his face, I was on top of my world. Even as I was given just one rule; never, never, never go riding on the trails alone. Never. The unknown forces are there waiting. The wothkins and the beelibump creatures. The big people, their eyes dark, their faces strained with purport, liked to repeat themselves. "Never go into the forest trails alone. Never. Anything can happen. Anything. Never.

"Agreed?" I agreed.

As a child I always agreed. As a child I agreed to anything they asked. Hardly hearing the latest instruction, I just agreed. It became my suit of armor. But then? I was a young kid, on fire to be up and out, and looking forward to this "anything."

This Saturday in May, I ride out alone to see where the trails go. Just to explore secret territory where scuffling sounds mingle with red vines growing up trees and hawks shrieking their joy. Birds everywhere, even walking under the stream water. Or upside down on the trees. Cottonwoods grow along the creek and swallows sweep up the air. Fear comes and then takes cover in this jig of creation which hums, buzzes, glides and seethes about me.

I ask Horse for a trot and then a canter. What happens is a falling. The trail is pulled out from under us. There is a sudden release and a catapult, right over his head, as the ground comes up and I lose him. On my back looking up to see, there are his knees and body poised above me, yes, falling towards me. That is all I know.

Then darkness. When my eyes open, the sky is sucking me up into its blue, blue dome. Breathless. Breathtaking. No breath. A deep quiet in my body. Voices then faces hanging over me, erasing the sky.

" She isn't breathing. Her lungs have deflated." A woman's voice. " Take a breath. Keep trying. I know it's hard but you must." The voice trembles. "Your lungs were squashed flat. Amazing he didn't kill you. Breathe deep."

The molasses in which I am swimming keeps me stuck. Paralyzed. What feels like two weeks-time scrolls by as I swim and swim, the sky waiting for me, stuck in a slow motion, turning me back inside, asking me to find my way out. Being held, and then, the push, and the sudden whoosh comes with a huge sucking noise, an explosion. I am popped back.

Breathtaking. Returned. Breath-filled.

"Your horse did everything not to fall on you. Look at him." Horse is chewing, looking at me, through bright eyes. Grass up to his knees.

"Where did he go?" She asks. "How did he miss crushing you? You must have an angel." The woman smiles knowingly as they hitch me onto his back while she holds one leg and we make a slow way back to the stable.

Angels. Soon my bruised chest is jostled by the gentle mahk-mahk sound of hooves meeting earth. The day smells of corn husks, fear, lavender and alfalfa.

Knowing is in the gut. Until that day, I didn't know I had angels. Or that one was named Horse. Until the breath was taken away, I didn't know it was there.

Knowing is instantaneous as that.

When God created the horse He said to the magnificent creature: I have made thee as no other. All the treasures of the earth lie between thy eyes. Thou shalt carry my friends upon thy back. Thy saddle shall be the seat of prayers to me.

And thou fly without wings, and conquer without any sword. Oh, horse. [5]

Why does Horse, my first master, deserve a poem? Perhaps it is because this chariot of mine brings up devotion and gratitude from so many. Horse, like the eagle, is a symbol of America and is a symbol of freedom. We use him for work, travel and sport. Yet, we see his essence as pure freedom.

Another reason is that now we know creation, in all it's many forms, as pure spirit and worthy of our respect. For they, the animals, have souls and purpose and are here to learn as they continue this journey. Just as we are learning what freedom truly means. — *EB*

Breathing with attention

1. Detoxifies and releases toxins from the body
2. Strengthens and boosts the immune system
3. Strengthens the heart, alleviates heart problems,
4. Alleviates and heals insomnia, panic attacks
5. Irrigates the brain, which improves memory & mental   capacity.
6. Massages your organs
7. Improves quality of the blood
8. Increases digestion and assimilation of food
9. Increases muscle tone
10. Allows the flow of prana (life-force) to radiate through all cells
11. Increases plasma prolactin (emotional well-being hormone) and decreases cortisol (fight/flight hormone)
12. Aids in overcoming addictions as it calms the nervous system
13. Elevates moods, raises your vibration
14. Relaxes the body/mind and relieves pain
15. Removes obstacles to the flow of life spirit/prana thru your being
16. Directly influences the involuntary (sympathetic nervous system)that regulates blood pressure, heart rate, circulation, digestion and many other bodily functions
17. Slows cellular degeneration which slows the decay of tissues
18. The breath rhythm is tied to the rhythms of the brain waves
19. Alerts the Vagus Nerve, the primary pacifying nerve in the body. Increased vagus nerve tone activates or quells parts of the body in need of calm or activation
20. Breath is a portal into Presence. Breath may be a portal into your True Self. "May" if you so choose. As a sovereign soul it is always your choice as to how you wish to experience this arising.

Make your home in the breath

We are born on the exhalation, and we receive the breath, receive rather than take. This breath is the foundation of the rhythmic flow of life force/prana throughout your being.

Instead of looking for ways to heal from the outside, you have everything you need to spark your natural healing and vital flow within. Right where you are, and right now.

*

There are only three ways in which the body releases toxins: Perspiration, elimination (peeing and pooping) and breath. It is the breath that releases the most toxins from the body's chemical reactions. Without a complete exhale do you see why there might be imbalances in health?

The 4-4-8 harmonious breath

Modern research and ancient Yoga masters both agree that a rhythmic, conscious breath where the exhale is longer than the inhale, not only regulates the heart but also stimulates and increases vital energy. It helps strengthen internal organs and thus regenerates and rejuvenates the body.

Yogic breathing or pranayam, has been shown to improve stress resilience. What you look for is a pattern that brings your breaths to around 4-6 breaths per minute. Classic Yoga breathing presents a 4-4-8 or 5-5-10 pattern. Feel it as a pause at top of inhale. Adjust the count for your own comfort. Breathing is a process, go slowly.

Sit upright in any sitting posture that is most comfortable for you. It is important to let the spine be straight.

You can also do this as a walking breath.

Close your eyes and begin to inhale / exhale deeply and slowly for three breaths. The 4-4-8 breath: inhale through the nose 4 counts. Pause the breath for a time. Exhale through the nose for 8 counts.

Anchor the exhale in the belly. Allow your attention to drop downward into the heart, solar plexus, low belly and then into the bones. Deeper now. Enjoy with an inner smile. As you

8

continue let the breath slow down to a steady and comfortable rhythm.

Then sit and embrace what is arising. Allow all with utter wonder and without attachment. If there is judgement? Allow that. Play with it. No resistance. Let nothing trouble the heart. This breath bears good fruit as you do it throughout the day. Notice and be alert.

Through conscious breathing, we allow the optimal functioning of the endocrine, nervous, digestive and other bodily systems, gaining mental and physical stability.

Research shows that Yogic breathing positively impacts mood. Studies show that Yogic breathing techniques reduce anxiety and depression. In part this is because yogic breathing practices stimulate the vagus nerve (which is part of the Parasympathetic Nervous System), and this effect ripples out to the body and brain, increasing neurotransmitters in the brain that reduce anxiety. [6]

Breathing in Nature is the ultimate and most invigorating of breathing ways. "In every walk with Nature, one receives far more than he seeks."[7]

The 4-4-8 pattern of breathing is what the yogis elucidate as a primal pattern. (I found some rishis who put forth 4-8-8; yet we are looking for comfort here. Everyday life calls for what is possible.) Researchers have found that it is this 4-4-8 pattern that stimulates the electrical rhythms of the heart, lungs, and brain, which become synchronized. They report that this breath rate can "induce up to a tenfold improvement in heart-rate variability," a measure of stress resilience. This pattern of breathing, done consciously, opens the capillaries to optimize blood flow, bringing more oxygen to the body.

The breath changes the physiology of the entire body.
It is the portal to more life, focus and greater alertness.
It is a portal to your True Self.

When the breath wanders the mind also is unsteady.
But when the breath is calmed the mind too will be still,
and the practitioner achieves long life.

Pondering:

Perfection

Allow it all to be exactly as it is.

Sit with the thought, "Everything is perfect. I look out onto a world that is innocent and perfect. This heart knows only perfection."

And in this day? Instead of trying to figure it out? I become a trust-it-all rather than a know-it-all. For that never worked for me.

I am here to allow all to arise and fade away. See thoughts, images, memories, sensations as coming from mystery and moving back into mystery. No need to follow them, simply allow them, embrace and trust them. Remember, the job of the persona mind is this flood of mind stuff.

Beyond all is truth

Whoever knows their Self, knows the Lord. [8]

Sages throughout history have brought us the wisdom of harmony and remembering our True Self. Their message? That the Divine and Its Creation are one. Reverence towards all life comes from realizing that there is only the Divine, there is only one ocean of Being. Nature is the shimmering presence of the the Infinite.

These breaths help us to relax into the heart, our deeper consciousness; they allow us to see into the fear and false beliefs that have manifested the world we see. Yes, the world.

These breaths help to calm the nervous system, to ignite our energy and to help us accept our fears and our griefs. These breaths help us age gracefully and relax out of guilt, anxiety and feelings of lack that come with false beliefs.

These are breaths that wash and aid the brain and memory and help us to remember compassion for all creation.

We are all being breathed and breathing together as the universe breathes us and sings its one song through us.

Breathe in the perfection of this moment right now.

As you sit you are:

Observing how the mind works (the persona/ego mind). All reactions, anxieties, images, inner conversations, thoughts, memories, all of it.

Releasing thoughts of "good and bad" and just accepting all the mind stuff that flows through the little mind, as flotsam in the ocean of awareness.

Realizing this; "I experience what I believe." Look at the life you have created through your beliefs. Do you even know what you believe?

Getting to know your false programs. For as I become conscious I continue to call people and events into my life that rattle my nervous system. They are here for a purpose. Nothing is without a purpose. Cancer is here to call us back to the truth of who we are.

It is the shedding of all the obstacles to acceptance, to trust, to love. I become love without conditions. In this way I allow the shimmering light of pure awareness (the Infinite ONE, to flow more fully through me. Yes, words can only point.

How to use this book:

The process: Breathing truly, deeply and with attention is a process; its gifts come with time and the willingness to use time differently. This book is for you so tear out pages and staple together into your own book. Make it your own. *All breathing practices* allow more energy, light and awareness to flow through the cells of the body. Enjoy!

Make a voice memo/recording of the breaths; play it to yourself as you sit. Your voice holds power for you.

Forgetting to breathe: you may notice that you forget to breathe or breathe solely in the upper chest. Give yourself two months to experience these new breaths before judging them. In time you will begin to feel more, feeling that is deeper than emotion. Attentive and rhythmic breathing takes you out of the persona mind. Go slowly.

Keep a journal. Write just a sentence or two each night as to how the breathing affects you. You are on a journey of remembering. Everything is important. As you relax, transformation occurs.

Soul School: You may come into a new experience of abundance; energy, love, wealth, creative ideas. Or you may feel an old sadness or rage; all are gifts from your indwelling spirit - what you need to awaken. It is always unique for you. Why? Because we each have different lessons to learn. This earth is a soul school. Here we live many lives, many dramas, many masters.

Every now and then twirl in a circle and say, "What an amazing soul am I." Be foolishness itself.

"Inhale the truth." For I would ask that you inhale the truths this book has to offer. When you read something that "quivers the bones", ponder it, breathe it in. For in this way you take truth into the very cells of your being. The Breath carries intelligence. This is paradoxical to the persona mind, yet pure truth to all who follow the breath.

The intellect takes in much that is dross or false. Why not take truth into the heart and lungs, into the atoms, the cells and the molecules of this, your life?

*

Breathing with attention illuminates down to
the cells of your Being. Right to Beingness itself.
It helps awaken the heart.
It is a key, a bridge to who
you are in truth and in reality.

The Mystery

Existence is an utter mystery that no one—not the greatest of philosophers nor the greatest of mystics has ever or will ever comprehend.

No one.

Not ever.

It is not a problem to be solved but a moment to be lived, played in and enjoyed.

It is given.

It is a gift.

Not for anything I have done but simply because

The Creator's desire is to manifest Love.

All creation is an extension of THAT.

You are an extension of THAT.

The body/mind noise

You may have noticed that the body holds tension in various places; there is "noise" in the body. Only corpses have no tension and no noise. Tension is a part of being in a body. You may feel this tension in the neck or the shoulders. You may carry it in the calf muscles or in the jaw.

You notice also that there is "noise" in the mind. There is a perpetual stream of thoughts, images, memories, fantasies, conversations, resentments, strategies and chatter that comes and goes. Where does this chatter come from? In truth? It is a mystery. In truth? It is not even yours. It arises. It is not a problem unless you follow these thoughts. Or believe them.

Do not believe your thoughts. Observe them.

Let them be. Let them come and go.
They are not good, not bad.

It is the persona's (ego's) job to keep a steady stream of images, thought, memories, fears, flooding through the mind. sometimes over 50,000 a day. Let them be as they are. Notice and smile.

Breath is life

When you allow yourself to take a deep breath and move into the space of peace, letting go of the restraints of thinking, you move into the place of possibilities. Here you bring into the light that which you wish to manifest.

You see it. You see it clearly.

You bring it into the embrace of Oneness.

You claim it. You know it. You live it. You feel it.

You vitalize it.

It will be made manifest right before your eyes. [9]

Be keenly attuned to the rhythm of your breathing, for it is breath that sets the tone of all your body's functions.

For most humans breathing is short and shallow. This is the breath of someone who is on alert, ready to fight or flee or freeze.

Begin to be attentive to taking long deep breaths as often as possible, for it is that type of breathing that informs the physiology and chemical reactions of the body that all is well and more. This offers a relaxed, alert state of mind that allows for feelings of safety and calm. The breath is a portal.

Remember.

Make your home in the breath

Breath

What is the Breath?

Breath is the body of God.   -Sufi

Breath is vital! Breath is the bridge to the divine within.
                                                    -Mystic Christ

Follow the breath; it will take you to the Paradise Land.
                                                    -*The Buddha*

Breath is the intelligence of the body.   -*Krishnamacharya*

The Breath is the physical manifestation of Holy Spirit in
the body mind.   -*Mystic Christ, Way of Mastery*

Without knowing the breath, a person is lost; wandering
about in the distractions of this world. Unknowing that right
where they are resides this treasure, this magnificent opening to
the Inner Kingdom of God, the bliss (deep peace) of Self-
realization.   - *Nityananda*

Breathing.

The word made flesh is a living word, not a scripture
but a breathing.
-Love's Body

Q: *What do we know for sure ?*
A: Right at this moment, 80 trillion cells of your body are
waiting for that nourishing wave of light/breath that feeds and
ignites your entire Being. You are one whole
and complete being.

Q: *What can we say for certain about the breath?*
Your body's metabolism circulation and ability to heal is all
dependent upon the rhythmic exchange of oxygen and carbon
dioxide. The flow of prana is enhanced by rhythmic breathing.
"Prana" is the Sanskrit word for the cosmic energy which moves
through all creation equally. Energy, light, consciousness, spirit,
are a few words that express it. It is the unseen ocean in which
life is. Prana or God -life is flowing through all that is.

Breathing and relaxation

> *The breath is always in the present moment. This cannot be said too often.*

A. Smooth, steady and calm breathing patterns help your body relax. These patterns stimulate the **parasympathetic nervous** system to lock in relaxation messages to your nervous system. This book will help you become aware of your breathing patterns and change them to bring positive benefits to your parasympathetic nervous system.

B. The **sympathetic nervous system** turns on, stimulates and locks in stress responses. This means that every time you hold your breath, gulp air or breathe spasmodically in response to negative situations you lock in stress and anxiety in the body and mind. your body becomes conditioned to frequently adopt a "fight, flight, or freeze," reaction. This activates your adrenal glands and tenses your entire body. Tension and stress are not in themselves bad or good. Yet, if it is a continual unconscious pattern it can be, finally, exhausting.

Breath and science

Both the ancients and modern research claim this truth: The slower, more complete and attuned breath leads to health and balance throughout your being. Let the exhale be longer than the inhale. It is not about gulping in more air; it is allowing the diaphragm to move and gently become more soft and open. This is often called belly or diaphragmatic breathing. You are attentive, you are the witness to the feeling sensation of the breath.

Notice if your exhale feels incomplete; many people forget to exhale. So let the exhale lengthen. Notice. Exhale completely.

Do this whenever you notice you are holding the breath, feeling jangled, impatient or frustrated. Watch what follows.

memoir - On the Bus

I travel by the light of flowers.
Just for the sake of traveling.   *-Basho*

South Carolina

I travel, as a child, from one grandmother to the other. Rosa, my mother's mom, lived outside Columbia and Geneva and Big Daddy lived on Sullivan's Island. Traveling by bus is always linked to butterflies and music. So it is to this day.

The music always begins with a waltz time, light and airy, like the Blue Danube. Geneva, my island grandma, is humming it in the old blue Chevrolet. We are on the way to the bus station. Tears rise in her eyes as she holds me quick while the cabbage butterflies tickle the bougainvillea. Once settled, and as the bus away, it is the pert blues hovering over the bright flowers which grow wild and untended in every field, from every shoulder of every road. Waves of hands, waves of sadness fill the window. But not for long.

Getting on the bus is tricky and takes fortitude and takes patience. It also takes a hand -up for me. Trading in the dimes and nickels for the ride is a gesture of initiation. While the women are making sure the packages are in hand, that the magic handkerchief and white gloves ("Lawd, have mercy, where is my handkerchief?"), there was the hustle as the children hid behind skirts, pulling faces while the men blew their noses to stave off the hugging cousins who came to give them away. It was an initiation into the unknown and excitement crackled the air.

Fathers, brothers, sons, all colors and ages, both black, white and other are alert and alive to the same anticipation, the

25

same searching for their chewing tobacco in the same high vest pockets, while everybody talked at once.

Bus riders shined up for the ride; the African American men had on hats and ties; the women wore bright colored dresses below their red lipstick. People painted themselves, curled their hair and looked smart. It was Sunday best with the picnic baskets hip close, the white gloves slapping the air and sailing with the words of good-bye. Sailing on the promise.

Seated, we all lapse into a marveling at having made it. Wasn't life a miracle? That we could roll over the countryside, be carried in God's own chariot, almost free of charge, and still eat our chicken salad? "Lawsy me, that's what they call Grace."

I sit towards the back with the window open. One of the few children, I feel safe. A child traveling alone, then, was not odd. And besides, there was no fear on the bus. To be on the bus was to be going somewhere and going in style.

Excitement and fear are different sides of the same coin; stop breathing and you are in fear. Breathe and you come into a state of excitement. On the roller coaster of life I can transform everything by simply breathing deeply and then? Riding on.

*

Further back in the bus come the humming strings, moving into a twelve bar blues, so sultry and lethargic and trailing off into little rifts on a harmonica as cooling as the bottle of my Dr. Pepper.

Bobbing alongside of us it is the dark-legged swallowtails and the hawk moths who joust in the trees and look for moisture in the leavings of cats and dogs, and on the sides of old houses where the humidity ends in drops of water. The

beetles were there but so hidden in shadows to rarely be seen; I
called them up because Geneva talked of them rolling balls of
earth round and round on the forest's floor while it was the
butterflies who came to play and dance and draw my
grandmother to say,

"We shall never know if there is a purpose to this grand
display, will we? Maybe it is just the play of God having fun. But
it gives us something to do, muse about it.'"

Those butterflies took to bobbing on the face of the sun
as the bus danced off the edge of the known world. By now we
are streaked with pink and purple swathed in the sun's lights just
as the teeth of the dark began to chew off the day. Twilight, the
in between, that time when the souls of those passed on play
on the edge of the sky. They arise; then, whirling and throwing
themselves at the light come the huge moths with their eyed
wings, which were there merely to wink at all those who follow
nature into her lair.

*

Traveling is also linked to corn and cotton fields burning
alongside the dusty shacks on which were painted the promises
of Schick razors, rolling tobacco, Buster Brown shoes and Coca
cola. There were bare bones houses and scrub pine forests in
which flickered moon flowers and Luna moths.

The bus is our world and is lurching faster now, throwing
off fumes and dust and anxieties, so much is being thrown up.
All of it, that landscape of the bus, is flowing into the red clay
bleeding up from wilting flowers in cracked asphalt, to black
women with their red and white bandannas and huge cotton
bags, to children with thin brown legs and faces pushing up,
faces running, turning the ground beneath them which rushes

27

away from me as they run, dream figures waving and shouting, calling us back.

Please come back. Take me with you, take me. Please.

Sometimes we catch each other's gaze and hold on as long as possible. Sometimes letting the eye streams turn to silk webs stretching out and stretching out, thinning until the eyes had to blink. All the broken gazes left hanging and glomming onto the particles of dust and sand which the bus throws out behind. A whirlwind of yearnings and byes and "come back"s, please. Everybody wants to be on the bus. We are the chosen people and we know it.

That's how I saw it clear as water then.

*

Blazing away from the dark corners of the night, away from the demons of the familiar, blessed through and through was what we were. We who had been lifted to roll and soar through the rutted streets, through the leaves of barley and the angel haired corn, through the clouds of midges which rose and fell as twilight came and fell.

We were wending our way to heaven because heaven was always someplace up ahead, around the next bend, and up and over that dell of scraggly oaks. We knew it; the songs proclaimed it. The blooded clay scattered into purple and pink as the salmon clouds swam into dark streaks and changed into dark smoke snaking through trees gnarly as witches arms.

No mistake about it, we were on the chariot of true grace. Things kept coming at us and peeling away; only the clouds kept up as did the moon, following us, holding us. For we were untouchable, a cosmic people alive with the rawness of creation at every turn.

28

I first heard the blues sung there in those buses by
singers who gave from their hearts for free and for fun.
Someone was always humming, guitar picking, then two more
joined and there is a small chorus. It may have been sad songs
but they would soon turn over into something else. Usually a
blues harp was brought out along with the fried chicken, potato
salad, cigar smoke, okra, cold slaw, lima beans and key lime pie
or vanilla custard all mingling in the steaming hum of deep
voices and sudden laughter.

Yes, this was a cosmic journey. As the night swallowed
up the sun the music sparked and cried out; we all felt held in
rhythms ancient as dirt.

Buses and trains had promises which lived on in songs
and the ever-present belief that surrounded all of us; we will
soon be in an elsewhere of timeless and unrelenting joy. I leave
that dried out me: those bills, that angry man, the bafflements
of life behind me. The promise of heaven and gardens of
delight was in the fumes of gasoline which funneled out as
wakes behind us and the long silver ribbon of road which
carried every expectation of love and acceptance, of waiting
friendships, of new faces welcoming as a mother's huge breasts
on which we will rest, finally. The power and fulfillment of our
dreams was up ahead.

Holy Road! Speak! Speak road of transformation and the
finding of the grail. And to this child the word "trip" always and
still rouses up angels and fried chicken and still holds up as
marvelous and fantastic.

It was a simple life on the bus yet it was moving with the
moon and stars along across the heavens. Everybody wanted to
give their legs up to the smoothing slide of it. It was the way of

taking on new power and knowing - for hadn't we all learned to give ourselves up to a melody?

A riff, a twelve bar blues riff, signaled that it was time for sinking within and letting go of all thoughts and worries? They were now elusive as the twilight butterflies; elusive, unreal. All worries. I knew it then on the bus; I forget it and must relearn it once again. And again. Hard headed. Stubborn. My father was right.

*

It is well-known that the Blues don't travel well in planes or Volvos but wear well in buses, trucks and station wagons. In the back of the bus the music gathers. I remember, I heard them telling it, "nothing good can come from Nazareth... how can anything good come from your own hometown?" It must be that the world is different somewhere else. Simpler. Wondrous as a film on a screen of silver and gold.

The changing skyline and the soft talk behind me of the sad, the erotic, or just plain bad doings of cousins and daughters, husbands and grandmothers, of wild cities and sad endings changed into starlit night and dark pines shooting into the night sky. Briny river sweat wafts from the lowland waters. I slept and awoke excited in the new minutes, talk and songs.

Family talk in my southern home was prevalent. Southern language is a close kin to a magnolia tree with those blossoms, fleshy and heavy, rising out of a dark bodice of wide leaves that shine in moonlight. Nothing is so soft and sensual as the whispers of southern girls or the lingering drawl of men as they hang their words on the pipe smoke and dip their faces together, talking of wild games and sassy women.

The words hang in the heat, the leaves emerge languid out of hot earth and long, unsleeping humid-wet nights. When a dollop of morning rain comes, the house breathes one long sigh of pleasures enthralling as dreams, elusive and promising a relief that never comes. The taste fills the cells as my uncles dress in vests with watches hanging from gold chains and the porches fill and the rockers rock and the tinkle of ice on glass.

The southern language is made to be chewed upon, it made for long deep silences in between the ambling drawn out sounds; its foundation is the heat burning earth, the fireflies sweet calls, endless sweat, endless critters, and belief in supper as balm to all the injustices of the world. And where's the best fishing? And can you smell the crawfish on that breeze? Always horses are racing somewhere and the keening of the doves calls out that death is close by, always the moving spell of life and death intertwined. Near at hand. But here, on the bus? No.

Through it all a high-toned rhetoric that keeps you spell bound. Tied up in low guttural sounds. And sighs. Nothing there is like those long, impenetrable sighs. To her dying day my mother could beat anyone in the length, depth and sheer surrender expelled in her sighs.

Later, I learn that in the small dusty towns of the share-croppers and the homesteaders, the bus brought relatives and news, packages and magazines, pictures of the world and hope. The migration of southern African Americans to the north was possible because of buses and trains, while I was just beginning my journey of bus and life, of moving from city to town to countryside, my first caravan. A time to be alone and unhampered by the giant people who looked at me as their project; freedom was my maple syrup.

The journey to somewhere lifted us into a shared wonderment. Once off the bus we fall into a smallness, decrepit even, some rumpled and worried, some wizened and pared down to bland. And joy, the dodger, the trickster, stayed on the bus. As Rosa, my Columbia grandmother, took my hand saying, "well, look at you, just look at you!" I spiral back to see it turn the corner, the huge *GREYHOUND* rushing behind the graceful blue dog. Bounding away, still he stays with me long, long after the bus has gone. While I, breathless, on the asphalt, wondering at all I am missing.

-eb 2008

The Bus Within

If worry rode that bus, he did not sit near me.

What I know now is that singing clears the mind field.

Song is simply music carried on the breath.

Past and future thoughts are banished as the breath/sound clears the body of cobwebs..

Later, I would look to sing with others. Music became a way, whether harmonizing, playing piano, listening or humming along.

Billy Holiday and I conjured up a deep melancholy as I did with Joan Baez. Edith Piaf was different; I asked her to give me the courage to belt out a song. Those folk songs were woven together with loneliness, yearnings, leavings and sad elegies.

Then came Bessie Smith, Ma Rainey, Eva Cassidy, Joanie Mitchell, Janis Joplin, and more.

Singing and chanting begins in the heart. I listened and learned to let songs move through, igniting happiness and blinding sadness and whatever else is hidden in this body complex. This alchemy of sound goes beyond thought or fantasy. While you never know, it may bring tears or take you into pure presence. Or cut a pathway in which spirit can peel back layers of wounds.   And the heart allows the love of the universe to play through.

Not Knowing

True awareness arises from a state of not-knowing. Even the most sincere investigation of self and spirit.... is often sabotaged by our tendency to grab too quickly for answers and ideas as we retreat to the safety of the known.[10]

The Know-Nothing mind

> *We are all napping in the world of the unexpected.*
>
> EB

> *We are here and it is now.*
> *Further than that all human knowledge is*
> *moonshine.*   -HL. Mencken

Some "Wonder questions" for you:

> *What is going to happen in the next three minutes,*
> *right where you are?*
> *Are you sure?*
> *How can you know?*

Enter stage left, Ann Elizabeth Hodges. She is sleeping; and since time is an illusion in which to play, it is November 30, 1954 and she is taking a nap on a couch in her home in Sylacauga, Alabama. A white dog is barking across the street. She wakes up suddenly, shaken, she is sure there has been an earthquake. Something burns her hip and leg. On the floor near her a fragment of rock lies smoking. There is a hole in the roof. What burst through her ceiling and landed on her hip? This same afternoon, when they tell her it is from a meteorite, and therefore, from outer space, "landsakes," is all she is reported to have said.

*post-note: Ann Elizabeth lived across the street from the Comet Drive-in. The universe has a great sense of humor. And there is nowhere to hide.

All human beings should try to learn before they die
what they are running from, and to, and why.   *- James Thurber*

Most of us are sleeping in a world of uncertainty. In a world of the unexpected. We are all living in the unknown.

And yet? We pretend to know lots.

We pretend to know what this life is about.

We plan.

We live in a future that is a fantasy in the mind, a past that is also an illusion of the little mind.

Underneath all our pretending to "know," our assured beliefs, our interpretations and preconceptions, our memories, our acting out, there is anxiety.

For in truth? Each of us knows that I don't know; who I am, what is my purpose, or even what this world is all about.

I don't know what it is I don't know.

What does it feel like to truly inhale this first step?

For me? It is like taking a breath of fresh, fresh air. Not being a know-it-all I can finally relax into being a trust-it-all. For trust is something I have had to learn; my childhood did not promote it as a given. Trust is the realization that I am not the doer or the maker of this life. A power is living through me. Perhaps. How much shall I open to this? How can I release my own resistances, my own fear, my beliefs?

To be in a state of not knowing is part of every spiritual tradition. Cultivating this "not knowing" collapses the persona mind. To actually cultivate this state, can lead to revelations. Before breathing, simply take off all beliefs about yourself; your name, your story, your beliefs or that you are "someone." Hang them in a closet somewhere. Then, give up all all future thoughts or plans. Strip yourself naked into this moment. Attentively notice what arises.

Listen. Feel. Sense.

The persona mind arises. Observe its thoughts, presumptions, resentments, ideas, conclusions. Observe and allow.

Return to not knowing.

The wisdom of uncertainty
Paradox is the foundation of the spiritual life
It seems paradoxical to the ego mind but not to the Self.

The wisdom of uncertainty
Sit with this: "I don't know what it is I don't know."
Alone in a room. In a crowd. While driving.
Do you know the true nature of anything? No.
You know the names of things.
You know what the can opener does, what the tree looks like.
Yet, their true nature, do you know this?
So, as you can see, it is the "wisdom of uncertainty," that is the
wisdom of all who desire to know their True Self. Perhaps it is the
beginning of true wisdom.
So I ask you to trust this step in becoming a bit more conscious.

A flute can only be filled with song when it is empty.

Realizing, that all along, I have known nothing at all about Reality (capital R) gives me a certain humility in the face of the mystery. This led me to the realization that I am not and have never been the master of this life.

Or in control of anything. Whether it is the weather, these emotions, these children, the world, the government, the future or the neighbor's goat.

Nada. Zilch. Nothing. Never.

Yet, pretending to be in control is a mighty big program for us infinite/finite beings, would you not agree?

When you don't know, you open up to a deeper dimension. Let go of knowing anything at all. Sit as the silence.

Make your home in the breath

Transformation

Breathing problems

After thirty-three years of teaching Yoga I have found that most people suffer from breathing problems. They breathe in the upper chest, mouth breathe, hyperventilate (quick breaths) forget to breathe or take shallow breaths. This reduces the oxygen and life force in the cells and leads to distress and chronic dis-eases. Yes, dis-ease.

For many? The diaphragm is frozen and the belly tight. Where does this lead? Forgetting to exhale, or a short exhale is rampant in our culture. This shallow breath weakens the organs of respiration and the lack of oxygen triggers a stress response. We are literally "holding our breath" while "fight, flight, or freeze," follows. A spiraling downward follows; all our bodily systems are disrupted by a unhealthy breathing pattern.

* Not fully exhaling causes carbon dioxide to build up in your lungs. This can cause you to yawn, make you sleepy or spaced out. The cells are starved for the electric and balanced oxygen/ CO_2 life force of the Breath.
* An excess of carbon dioxide also decreases the amount of oxygen available to your cells which react in the following ways: your arteries start to contract, causing your airways to constrict, which in turn causes you to hold your breath. This leads to an increase in tension and a cascade of stress responses into a downward spiral. Both yogis and modern science agree: The quicker we breathe the sicker we become.
* *A breath of radiance is soft, long and witnessed.*

Begin by changing the mind ,

given that your

thoughts

are

powerful

beyond belief

As you awaken in the morning state this: "I am awake. I am embodied. I am anchored to this earth. I am one with the Infinite."

And, then, best of all, "My Presence is a blessing to all creation!"

When you can say this without smirking, when you say it with wild enthusiasm, you are on the way to accepting the truth of who you are.

Breathe this in and then?

Make your home in the breath

You are a sovereign soul

You are 100% responsible for this life - all events, thoughts, and actions.

You are a sovereign soul and yet? You can choose to be a victim. It is always a choice. Being a victim is a powerful program here. The mind is that powerful. The power to choose is divine. Fear or love. Blame or trust.

The victim says, "the world is responsible for my unhappiness and for my failure; my parents, the schools, the Chinese fortune cookies, bad dogs, too much rain, the President and of course the cost of everything. All have held me back."

I will look for someone to squeeze love from. I will look for a leader who will make me more money. I will make lots of money and be famous; I will find objects, people, things, beliefs, sex, fame, memories and drugs to make me happy. I will then feel no lack or fear. Then? I will find happiness."

Timeout for a really good laugh here, and a pause. It never happens. Pleasure based on the world and its dramas, based on objects, other people, money and fantasies come and go.

In truth? Your experience is never sourced from anything outside of you. Ponder this. You are 100% responsible for this life - all events, thoughts, and actions. You are the master of the moment. How do you wish to experience this moment?

43

Truth sets you free
But first? It will piss you off.

Breathe with attention and claim the truth:

"I and I alone am responsible for this life. Nothing and no one outside of me sources my experience. I will experience what I believe."

"I have never been a victim of the world. I have all the powers of Heaven and earth."

"I am here to create consciously."

"I am able to choose and create a life of abundance, freedom and love."

"I and the Creator are One."

As you breathe the truth into the cells of the body, shifts take place in the core of your being. Do you see?

This is a way of moving into stillness to experience your True Nature. Heaven is another way of expressing the same thing, and Reality is another.

Change.

Breathing with full attention and claiming the truth raises the frequency of the body, the very cells. Acceptance is a high frequency, love is a very high frequency.

What else raises the frequency? Dancing, singing, laughing and choosing thoughts of allowance, trust and love. Gazing into the eyes of a friend.

Be curious as to what is happening around you. Smile. Laugh. Say, "Yes. In this moment it is all perfect, no matter what is arising. It is not serious."

Here is the best part; whatever is arising is on the way to changing even as you observe it, so feel and breathe. This is a plane of change.

Change is the reality here on this earth plane.

What is it about you that does not change?

It is all perfect

Yes, it is all perfect
Everything that comes to me has been called by me.
How can it be other?
The spark of the Infinite one at the core of my
consciousness knows exactly what I need to take the next step.
Remember to simply say, "yes" within.you.
Yes, to everything. "Yes, it is all perfect. Thank you for this coffee
and this car and these bills. Nothing is unacceptable to me. I allow
all to be as it is, moving through me and this world I create
through my beliefs,
I allow all to be as it is."

Feelings

The breath is tied to feelings.

If you bring forth what is within you, what you bring forth
will save you. If you do not bring forth what is within you,
what you do not bring forth will destroy you. [11]

When you begin to allow the shadows of the past that
dwell as thorns in the body to be seen, this is healing. As you sit,
as you breathe, as you invite the fear, the memories of old hurts,
the resentments, the feelings of lack, to be brought up from the
dark cave, this is healing. For as you shine the light of your
awareness, the light of your acceptance, those shadows cannot
find a hiding place.

It takes great courage to truly feel all feelings. The truth of our feelings frees everyone to be authentic; frees everyone to be real. When you express, feel, embrace your feelings you allow others to do the same. Then? We can laugh together.

Denied emotions hide in the molecules of the body. Denied feelings lead to anxiety, depression and self-hate. Allowing them, as threads of energy, frees us. No matter how much fear arises, be with it all.

Denial of true feelings and the repression of true feelings leads to much suffering. The nervous system contracts, the blood vessel constrict, the flow of hormones is stunted, the whole being closes down like a fist. The very flow of life force shuts down. You are here to explore the universe, for transcendence and for the unfolding into greater depths of love and enthusiasm. What do you choose?

Beliefs are changeable. Who I am, at one level, is my feelings. Once those are denied then connection, intimacy (into-me-see) is cut off. A denied feeling grows in magnitude within and results in knots of bitterness, guilt, rage, frustration taking root in the very cells of the body-mind.[12]

Abandonment

Who has not felt abandonment?

If, as a child, you had a parent who looked into your eyes and said, "You are perfect. You come from pure love. You cannot make a mistake. Follow your passion to know your Self. I am always here to support you. What you desire will be, so want the highest good for you and for everyone. You cannot fail." If you had a parent like this, then, you are ahead of the game.

The experience of abandonment has closed many down. Parents in fear could not love you unconditionally. Their parents forgot how to love them. They could not reflect back to you your magnificence as an expression of the Infinite.

In truth? You are love in form and you came here to know yourself and to remember your true nature.

When you allow the, of not being seen, of not being loved, to be embraced rather than resisted, your life changes completely. As you face your anxieties you notice the shadows slipping away. Your life is now effortless and abundant. You are the vessel through which the Divine one flows, guides and reveals itself as you and to you.

Repression of feelings and war

In the world of psychology and now in the world at large, repressed anger is seen as the most destructive and dangerous of all human emotions. We human beings are quite good at turning our repressed anger in towards ourselves. We are also quite learned at inflicting this anger on others, as the Nazis did. "I don't like myself so I shall find others to carry this burden of self-hatred."

Turning it on ourself leads to angry self-criticism, ruthlessness, guilt and feelings of impotency. All because one cannot bear to own up to feelings of anger! All of this leads to dis-ease in the body, rigidity, early aging and anxiety.

Repressed anger lies at the root of severe mental disorders, such as obsessive compulsive behavior, schizophrenia and psychotic breaks.

Using the breath and allowance of all feelings many people have come out of severe negative mental states. We know now that it is this repressed anger turned outward that is the cause of all wars, conflicts and aggression.

Ready to love what arises as feelings?

Until I truly take 100% responsibility for everything that is what I call my life, I stay in victimhood. I give away my power. As I take responsibility I take back my power. For if I depend on others, events, objects, gold coins to make me happy, they can also take away my happiness. I know this so well in my own life. I expected a marriage to bring me safety and happiness; it brought such pain and guilt that I had to face myself and my expectations. Finally ask the question; what is this life, this existence truly about?

I remember first hearing that failure is a great blessing in this world. After many failures I am forced to reflect on life, truth, reality. I let go of needing a man and set out poor in the eyes of the world, to live without beliefs. To greet each day unknowing but expectant, this became a kind of path for me.

As I begin to breathe deeply and feel into my heart, belly and solar plexus, the body always talks to me.

Now? I am ready to listen.
Resisted feelings are the ego's playground.
I begin to feel my way to the soul.
Breathing is allowing all feelings to be felt completely.
They are simply old energy patterns asking to be accepted, liberated and moved through.
Even rage is a path to power. As long as I blame no one.
As long as I take 100% responsibility for what is
under my
skin.

Resisted feelings persist and cripple us.

Make your home in the breath

Pondering: (A repeat here.....it is that important.)

Nothing you experience is sourced outside of yourself. Nothing. Your happiness or suffering is not caused by the parents, society, the government, the world or God. When you take 100% responsibility for your life, you take your power back.

You are a master. You are no longer a victim. Yes, it takes diligence. It takes a willingness to take back your projections and perceptions of others. The best thing is? I began to eat them for lunch. All the judgement thoughts I have of another? I take the finger back and point it at my own heart. What is it I refuse to own in myself?

When you realize this everything changes.

You are given choice in each moment for acceptance or judgment.

Do you see? Once you free yourself fully from the net of victim consciousness, you inherit a full dignity. And take back the power you are gifted from simply being born.

Rage is love as a tornado.

Reflect on this. Express those feelings you once thought were "bad." Anger claimed and expressed brings us into our power. It is all a neutral event. Just make sure you own all feelings as yours. Blame no one and see how it feels to be free.

Weather and feelings

Like the earth there is weather that must move through us to cleanse and balance our inner self. The earth uses storms and tidal waves and earthquakes for cleansing. In allowing this flow, in this allowing, the body /mind heals and expands into true health. It is in attuning with this flow of cosmic light, (feelings, prana, consciousness) that brings balance, insight and mastery.

Breath & Science

The ancients and the modern researchers agree:

Three things that effect the Heart:

-Yogic or diaphragmatic breathing with attention

-A lengthened exhale

-Taking longer but fewer breaths; look for 4-6 breaths per minute

Breathing with attention and its effect on the heart

"Where your attention goes, energy flows." This is a well-used directive from Yogis and spiritual masters from all cultures. When we breathe with the heartbeat you bring your devotion (attention) to your heart.

There was a time, during the 80's and 90's, when a number of Olympic athletes were dying of heart attacks during their early 50's or 60's. Shock ran through the athletic culture; were these Olympians not the prototype of radiant health? Questions led to a new way of working-out called interval training. *The nature of the heart is that it needs time to integrate intense exercise with a rest period.*

The heart, they found, responds to brief periods of effort, running or fast walking for 6-7 breaths, followed by a period of walking or resting for 6-10 breaths, followed by another pulsing of effort for 6 breaths and then rest. Many coaches call for eight of these cycles three times a week for a good work-out. It gives the heart a workout which leads to coherence rather than stress. The body looks for effort and flow and then rest. It leads to what medical experts call HRV or Heart Rate Variability. Yoga involves a kind of interval effort and rest.

Slow Breathing is a Sign of Health

Once you go below 10 breaths a minute you start to engage the parasympathetic nervous system and this relaxes the body when it has been injured. When it is out of balance. Slow breathing activates the vagus nerve, the primary cranial nerve, which is associated with a recuperative state.

A person who is breathing at four breaths a minute will only breathe about 5,760 times a day. This is healthy. At the "normal" breathing rate of eight breaths a minute that count doubles to 11,520 breaths a day. At 16, which is still slow for many, that rate reaches to 23,000 breaths a day, (a sign of illness.) At 25 breaths a minute, we are clipping along at 36,000 breaths a day, which is a far cary above a normal rate.[13]

Virtually all compromised people (asthma, bronchitis, heart disease, diabetes, cancer, etc.) have accelerated respiratory patterns. During rapid breathing carbon dioxide becomes deficient, oxygen delivery to the cells is reduced, breath-holding time is reduced, and the natural automatic pause is absent in each breath.[14]

HRV

Perhaps more important, slow breathing increases <u>heart-rate variability</u>. HRV is a measurement of the fluctuation in heartbeat during an activity. This measures how flexible the heart is, how able to find balance after activity or stress. "If your heart rate fluctuates at 60 to 80 beats per minute, cardiac-wise that's healthier than someone whose heart rate varies between only 70 and 75 beats per minute. It means your system is not so rigid... Lance Armstrong has a massive swing in heart-rate variability.... an unhealthy or older person has a much smaller one. The way to increase variability is to breathe slowly." [15]

You are given a certain number of breaths when you come into the manifest world. The elephant breathes three breaths a minute and lives for over a hundred years. Birds breathe quickly and live short lives. It is well to slow down the breathing.

- *Yogic breathing or pranayam,* has been shown to improve stress resilience. What you look for is a pattern that brings your breaths to around 4-6 breaths per minute. Check your own pattern throughout the day. Simply bringing your attention, which is your devotion, to the breath, slows it down.

- *A person breathing at four breaths a minute* will only breathe about 5,760 times a day. This is healthy and leads to balance to all systems of our being.

- *Yogic or diaphragmatic breathing strengthens the heart,* and leads to greater HRV and coherence. This means that the heart is able to adjust more easily to various intensity and rest periods.

Yogic Breathing

Deep belly or Yogic breathing not only regulates the heart but also stimulate and increase vital energy, strengthen internal organs and thus regenerates and rejuvenates the body. Through breathing consciously, we can achieve the optimal functioning of the endocrine, nervous, digestive and other bodily systems and gain mental and physical stability.

When your exhale is longer than your inhale, the vagus nerve sends a signal to your brain to turn up your parasympathetic nervous system (PNS) and turn down your sympathetic nervous system.(SNS). The sympathetic system commands our fight or flight response, and when it is stimulated it increases heart rate and breathing, and increases stress hormones like cortisol.

The parasympathetic system controls your rest, relaxation, and digestion response. When the parasympathetic system is dominant, your breathing slows, your heart rate drops, your blood pressure lowers as the blood vessels relax, and your body is put into a state of calm and healing. (Appendix includes research websites)

Heart Chakra

The heart chakra is the center through which all energies must pass. It is located at the base of the sternum in the chest. A chakra ("Wheel") is a vortex of energies which meet and help distribute cosmic life force through the body.

The heart chakra is associated with the Astral Body and the rose color of love. Spiritual energy must pass through the heart to be transformed to physical energy. Physical energy will transform to spiritual as it exits through the heart chakra. All thoughts, emotional experiences, all hurts, and fears, are filtered through this chakra.

The heart knows only abundance of love, of happiness, of gold coins, of compassion, of tenderness. For they are all connected, all one stream of energy. The heart knows only unlimitedness, spaciousness, abundance, peace, safety and eternity.

The Heart

All loving thoughts are true. All thoughts of resentment, all projections of blame of judgement are from the persona mind. You are the master of the mind.

The heart generates the largest electromagnetic field in the body. It has been found that these fields permeate every cell of our being. These fields seem to act as a synchronizing signal for the body in a manner analogous to information carried by radio waves. Further, this energy is not only transmitted internally to the brain but is also detectable by others within its range of communication.

If the heart has been hurt due to emotional or physical abuse it is a good practice to breathe into the heart.

All breaths done with awareness and intention help to balance the chakras; this allows cosmic life spirit to flow and radiate equally throughout your being.

The Heart

*When the dawn of love floods your heart with it's beauty
all else fades into nothingness.*   *-Anandamayi Ma*

Awakening the heart is for you and all creation.

Summon the power of positive feelings.

Reconnect with all that is good and life affirming in your

daily life, the sun and the moon, the food and water, the friends.

Someone smiles at you. A friend calls to say hello.

A Prayer of gratitude beyond all others

Great Spirit, Infinite One, Beloved, Lord,
Thank you for this life. This life is your life,
We are one.
Thank you, thank you, thank you, thank you.

The Heart

What is there in the jar that isn't also in the river?
What can you find in the house that is not in the city?
This world is the jar, the Heart the river;
This world is the house, the Heart the city of miracles.[16]

Let the heart/mind emanate this love from your being.
With each in-breath say, "I breathe in light. With each out-breath,
I breath out love." With this you bless all creation.

This is our only purpose here, to love and to bless all
creation.[17]

"What shall I do now?" is a prayer, for it is the question, along
with the breath, that creates a space. Continue to breathe and
notice how this brings you out of the fear and anguish of the small
self, and ignites the wisdom of the holy Self.

*All human beings should try to learn before they die
what they are running from, and to, and why.* James Thurber

Columbia, South Carolina

"Your great grandmother used to stand on her head," my father mentioned in passing as we both hunkered over our pecan pancakes. He is ladling on the maple syrup, grinning, while shining on me his big white sweet tooth. I was playing with the food. All the while hanging on his word pictures.

"She holds her petticoats and skirt between her legs, fastens her eyes at the end of her nose, and hangs there for thirty minutes at a time."

I chewed on in exquisite silence. Imagining her oval green-eyed face emerging a fearless red and radiant. I noted my father isn't smiling. "She was waiting up for me - to smell my breath. She didn't like beer, wine, vodka, martinis or anything really good and fun. Wasn't her standard. "

About his family he rarely spoke. I fastened myself to his face. With his great Irish good looks and his long involved stories he could crack a crowd open into laughter and hold them in the center of his palm for as long as he wanted.

How much I envied this talent of his. I was about nine years old and to hold even one person captivated for the length of a knock-knock joke was beyond magical.

He inspired listening. He looked like Tyrone Power, so he inspired looking. My parents were born between world wars and they grew up during the depression. They loved working hard, jazz, dancing all night, drinking scotch, eating oysters and playing tennis. At their parties drinks and cigarettes flowed, and the stories grew more ridiculous and meaner as the night closed over them.

*

A smile started to bloom but, seeing his face fall, I chewed it back along with a mouthful of orange juice. That he was holding back a torrent of pain and denied feelings would become known to me later, when I no longer lived at home; when I returned with the eye of the explorer and with my own heart wary of him and of handsome men in general.

"What else, Dad?" I asked.

"I would come home late at night from a date and there she would be, in the corner of the main room. On her head. Skirt everywhere. Pantaloons covered her legs, starched and pleated."

"Did she have ruffles and bows?"

"Her? No." Incensed at the thought. "What are you talking about? None of the women in our family, except your mother, know how to wear bows or elegant things. Ruffles. No, there were no bows in any part of her."

Wrapped in old jeans, scruffed up tenny-runners and a shredded tee-shirt with dabs of yesterday's oatmeal and raspberry jam over the heart, I felt his concern. Crumbs on my lips I licked my mouth slowly, hoping he wouldn't see. I wanted to get out of the house. No bows or ruffles anywhere. He looked sad. Like he had forgotten the last words to Kubla Khan all over again. I felt his hurt and had a new necessity to chew on, this learning to wear bows. If only to make my father smile. Making him happy became a game; one exhausting, impossible game.

*

Sure and stern and without vanity of any kind, this was all I knew of this great grandmother. She was a southern woman with no sense of needing to conform or to please anyone at all. I came to admire her from afar. Had he not lived with her, had he not felt her striving for his perfection, he might have also admired her. Close up she must have been as ferocious and inexplicable as the Asian Viper, a poisonous snake I had just read about.

There are those questions, captured in a child's mind that continue to spark and ebb. Without resolution or adult interest as the little mind is a wave of questions. Did she try to pass that fierceness on to us? A disdain for appearances and a spirit of teaching all children they are meant for greatness? Did my father run fast away from the women in his family to find that something just beyond reach, something else entirely? Or are we all born as wanderers and must then learn to root, as a plant or a captured band of horses must learn to let go of fear and get along with others? Survival is one thing. Awakening something else entirely.

Rooting was not my father's way. His chariots were fast and his heroes comedians and baseball players. His gift of laughter was a true gift. He came out arms reaching to embrace the new, whether it was TV or Sid Caesar, Edsels, a face of celebrity, or the latest popular Sinatra song. He wanted to see the world and the city lights and leave his name where it could be seen. HIs discomfort with domestic life, with houses and with women wove a concoction built on a need for more and different work every two years. It became his blueprint for life.

Perhaps, in looking from this angle of the sun, there was a method to it; to give us girls back that kingdom of caravans. And the motto: "Don't get too comfortable." I made a fortress in my bedroom, a camp impregnable to outside peering eyes. My freedom was in an army of projects: drawings, science experiments (can one still see a lighted lamp bulb under a sheet and two blankets? And if left forgotten what outcome? Burning, a fire, a dragging of the mattress into the street amid screams and curses.). There was a collection of snakeskins, insects, turtle shells altogether under the bed, waiting for a plan.

We moved.

We merged with a migrant tribe moving and rediscovering a landscape of highways, and tracks, a country of vast fields and forests, of huts and mansions, mountains and plains, of cities and towns. As I read our history, I see that humans have always been wayfarers. Settling in one place is a relatively new path; in truth we are more gypsy than settler. Move on, my father said and we did. We followed kicking, sullen and hating to leave the sweet haunts of the south for the acid air of New York. Still, the clouds and the moon kept up with us on the Silver chief as we careened towards our new landing place. Always unknown. And therefore? It might just be paradise.

*

I wonder now if my great-grandmother had read books on Yoga. How else would she know how to do this inverted pose? This headstand? Or how would she know that it was something that might be good for her? Or did she do it to be contrary - as were many of the southern women I came to know and love - when her husband came and then walked out? It is said that she started the first private school for African American children in South Carolina. It would have been like her.

Still, "There you are." As Geneva, my father's mother, would say, eyes ablaze, ending all further discussion.

Determined, Virginia, my great grandmother, reminds me of a suffragette standing upright, bare of jewelry, pomp, pretense and make-up, with that same gray and brown smocked blouse, hair a nest of wisps and bobby pins, mostly unsmiling. Yet, in this one photograph, her smile stretches from the England to Kansas and her hands are holding my child/ father, as if he was the most precious treasure given to womankind.

Mother love. I wonder now, did she take this love and make it into a quilt and lay it out over this earth, onto all the children of the world? Who knows anything for sure? I trust it is so; for it is how women live when they are conscious and awake. When they know that all people are children of the Infinite One, and therefore, brothers and sisters.

Life was hard then as now for a single woman without a family; and back then there was no day-care. My paternal great -grandfather was a railroad man and spent much time away from home. He may have even left his family. All we know is that he fell off the family tree, his name disappeared from their lips and his story is only a sentence.

It may be that Virginia took away his gin or hid his scotch one too many times. Alcohol was, to these southern women, not just bad, it was the devil's elixir. It would rot the mind, melt the will, twist the intestines, destroy the toes and the family, and leave a person lying in the dirt in their underwear talking gibberish.

Geneva and Rosa, my mother's mother, both decried television. "Its silly and without any moral purpose. Not worth the words to talk of it." Popularity meant nothing to them and they saw how television and movies can be like drugs and alcohol. Geneva often said to me, "Ask yourself how you want to spend the time you are given here. Always good to ask. So there you are."

That there was a chemical/brain imbalance in our family line is easy to see. The Irish side and the French side and probably some unexpected ancestors alongside. It marked us, yes. But then? After the war, the culture was out for broke, out for excitement. And everyone has these marks from wrestling with the world, don't they? As a friend says, "Everyone lives with a banged up heart."

*

Both my grandmothers were bird-dogs. They sought to keep alcohol out of their men in ways both nefarious and unrefined. Geneva, her eyebrows cocked for battle, emblazoned in her rightness, followed my grandfather to his mates' houses to check if they were tippling. She would stand overly erect and so sure of her judgments as he hid from her to enjoy his evening drink of wine. On his deathbed, she finally relented and took him some wine to ease his pain. In most everything she knew what was right - and had no fear of sharing it. "I am right and know what is best for everyone," is a program old as the hills. I see it in myself and? I shudder.

Always, I feel a bond with my great-grandmother. It is all about liking the headstand and being alert to not looking for approval from others. Yoga brought me into the body and allowed it to talk to me. Yoga is truly a way of incarnating in

69

the body fully. From there and I saw how many people lived above the neck - or even outside of the body. This river of life Edgar Cayce talked o, so many talked of, all looking to immerse within it's Godstream. Clearly, I had been "otherwise involved," most of my life.

All around me I saw people on hold, embracing the world and its dramas. But, here is the problem; the world always holds up another goal to obtain, another problem to solve. In the end and in the beginning, it is all about choices, in each moment. To remember who I am is a breath to breath remembrance.

*

My father said she stood on her head out of boredom. But she was a reader and a thinker. She knew about Yoga, the Vedas, and the East with its unique take on the weaving of the Soul. She knew that it may take a few lifetimes for a person to awaken. Or it can happen in an instant. In truth, each awakens in their own unique and unexpected way. Let me be clear, as I continued I knew I was tapping into my true nature, the Godstream. So what can be more worthy than that? What, I asked myself? If you want freedom above all else? Name it. Say it out loud. Listen to yourself. To know thy Self is my only purpose here. All else flows from this.

This loving of the headstand, of breathing and of turning within may go far back in the family tree; only no one talked about it. There were other topics untouched at the family table: God, sex, money and feelings. Yes, the big four. On the subject of the body and headstands there was a definite taboo. For wasn't India a heathen country? A country of poverty and dusty roads going nowhere?

70

*Great
Grandmother

Instead of
resisting change,
surrender. Let life
be with you, not
against you. If
you think 'My life
will be upside
down' don't
worry. Upside-
down may be
better than
right side up?

*

At an early age, and enthralled by southern stories and southern literature, I saw life's possibilities. Books became precious to me. They were my night window on the world. I came to admire a passel of other women: Eudora Welty, Karen Blixen, Margaret Rawley, Rachel Carson, Bessie Smith, and Carson McCullers. By the time I was eighteen, I had read everything I could find from Faulkner to Kierkegaard to Tennessee Williams and John Steinbeck, from Hemingway and Thomas Wolfe to the enigmatic stories of Flannery O'Connor. In the nuclear family I felt a loneliness and a claustrophobia.

Writers and musicians called out.

In richly layered novels, here were the most provocative and talented southern women without outlets for their passions, their deep feelings, their insights. They resorted to drink, insanity, wild partying, raising peacocks, running naked through streets, zealotry, suicide, obsessions, and now, standing on their heads. I felt their lostness. I felt their deep pain. I felt their not being seen. I would come to know them as life called me to move and move again. We had already left the south for a new house in the north. Then the west, then the midwest.

Sometimes, marinating in the hormones and inexplicable passions of teenage-dom I would feel these beings parade around my bedroom; they illumined my world as a circus in which we all performed. I dreamt of gymnasts doing somersaults on the backs of bulls and horses. It was a foretaste, for later, I would see them in the Etruscan paintings in an Art Class at college. Soon, I came to know this world as a huge stage. We play our roles and learn to play them well; until we realize they are roles.

What caught my eye as a young girl was how wounded people looked. It was in their eyes. A look of shutdown. Walking down a New York street, few did not look wounded or damaged or on the verge of a breakdown. Even half dead. I began to see women in truth. In books and in life I saw how many projected their power and their vision onto men who were made into heroes. I read about the lives of women in India, in South America, in Iran.

My women's college was loyal to women's freedom, to thinking rationally and to giving back; freedom, it was said, includes great responsibility. The Peace Corps called many of my friends as Kennedy asked, "Ask not what your country can do for you. But ask, what you can do for your country." It was a time of asking that question. And following through.

*

Throughout the routine of my life there was an ever present urgency to escape. But to where and when? This urgency was fired by something else; a distinct belief that I was not here for long. Held somewhere in the matrix of this self was a parable; "gather while you can, all the pretty horses of experience, for you're on the way out." This inner surety kept watch over choices I made. I was passing through faster than others. Fueled by this, any purpose was to be lived quickly. This angelic drummer beat out her message; this earth plane is a short ride so take in it's enchantments and be alert.

I left college and my days were spent in art, singing, teaching and wandering through forests. Asking the question 'where is this heaven?' And what is this existence all about, really?" This life I saw around me felt shallow and tight and unconscious. I viewed the family from a distance. And went my own way. As everyone must. To live from the past may mean to live from the world's values. Other people's values. While your own soul is giving you clues, and showing you another way entirely.

Suffering

When you feel unseen, when you feel that no one understands you or cares about your feelings or your sadness. When life is overwhelming, and when your days are full of responsibilities that only add frustration. When you question if there is a purpose in life and you want to get off this earth. Breathe. Breathe. Allow what needs to come up, come up.

Breathe. Breathe. And then drink in the Light and the love of the Father/Mother God, the Source of all. Know that you are in a sea of love and Light. Allow yourself to feel immersed in it, and feel yourself to be expansive, unlimited Light.[18]

HIlda Von Bingen said, "We are feathers on the breath of God."

Mankind's unhappiness comes of his greatness; it is because there is an Infinite in him, which with all her cunning she cannot quite bury under the finite. [19]

If I am living through the filter of the persona mind I am in suffering, I am caught in a belief in separation. Awakening from this is not an event but a remembering, a revelation or revealing of what has always been. I just had my attention elsewhere.

We are bubbles floating in this Sea of Awareness. Which is Spirit. Which is Love. Which is God. -EB

Q: What is the cause of all suffering?

A: It is the belief in separation. Separation from the ground of all being, the Infinite Birther of the Cosmos. It is the belief in the separation from that, my true nature, my infinite Self. It is a belief in separation from the earth and separation from others.

It is the belief that I am a body/mind that will sicken, suffer and die. From this belief in separation comes an identification with the body/mind rather than with the unlimited experience of the infinite one. Pure awareness.

From oneness with the Infinite I fall into a limited fearful false self - the persona or ego self.

Only when plunged into grief did I choose to turn and truly peruse the mind and my self. Before that? I wailed without contemplation, without reflection. Suffering brought me out of unconsciousness.

Suffering leads to deeper reflection on existence.

There was an ancient holy woman, in a village in India, who became exhausted by listening to the terrible suffering of the village people who came to her for healing. So, one day, she asked during her meditations, "Divine Mother, Heavenly Father, you certainly have the ability to take away all suffering. So why not just do it? We would all be so much happier."

God answered her, "Then they would continue to live this gift of life out of selfishness, intolerance and ignorance. They come to you and you let me heal them through you and you tell them who they are, you tell them of their Creator. They begin to have gratitude and to forgive themselves and others. They begin to talk with me. How would they wish to know truth without suffering?"

Many sages agree. True wisdom is not always acquired by teachers and reading; it is often through pain and suffering that a new vision of reality arises. Being stopped in my tracks draws me inward. Unless I am in resistance. Here, I would add, grief also leads me to my own heart. Suffering may bring us to realize that most human-beings suffer. In this, we know compassion for we realize our oneness even before our True Nature is revealed to us.

77

Pondering:

After a breath, allow the feelings to arise. If there is doubt, confusion, jealousy, guilt, anger, grief, resentment or whatever, ask this wonder question:

Q: *If love allows all things, embraces all things, trusts all things, how does it feel to sit and allow?*

Breathe into the feelings allowing them to grow. Say, "I am willing to feel this energy completely. Bring it on."

Sit and feel and allow whatever feelings arise. Allow the feeling you call "suffering" to arise. As you allow all to arise - jealousy, guilt, confusion, sexuality, doubt, resentment, you are allowing old karmic energies to be embraced. Play with them and know they are not who you are.

Notice where it is in the body. Notice if it moves as you sit and observe. Feel it as a thread of energy. Be diligent. You are here to feel it through to completion. That may be five minutes or an hour.

Notice, does it change as you allow it to be?

Love without conditions.

Love accepts all things, allows all things, embraces all things, trusts all things. And thereby transcends the world.[20]

Love without conditions means, literally, to embrace the darkness of the sub-conscious. When I first heard this, the quintessential teaching of Jesus and so many masters from the east and middle east, I felt a rock in my heart.

Q: *And does that mean my brother who belittles me or the politicians who let logging companies destroy the Redwood forests? EVERYONE?*

A: It doesn't mean you condone their acts; it means you understand how they might be as they are. Their fear. Their feelings of lack. They may have been unloved. They must have great fear. Will you look through their anger to the light that shines through the eyes?

I already knew that my judgements, resentments, blames and hatreds, affect only me. All thoughts take on a form. Given that they begin in this, my consciousness, they actually boomerang back and attack me. I 'project' onto others what I refuse to see in myself. Every judgement is an attack. [21]

In the end? It is never about them but about you; the baggage you choose to carry that squashes the heart. See everyone as a soul and a student of life. Each is looking for love in his own way. Each has a unique flavor. Do you know your sister's purpose here? Perhaps it is to raise the dust or challenge your patience? Or bring up your frustration to be seen and therefore, healed. In the end? It's not about her or him but about you.

Love without conditions

My dharma was to teach. Your dharma is your own purpose and intention in the world. As long as it erupts form your happiness.

"Do not work out of duty. Even if you serve others. Do what you do joyfully or do not do it.....for if you do it in the spirit of sacrifice it is not a gift to the world or to yourself....nothing prospers that does not come from love." [22]

To see another as a mirror of your own self grounds you in truth. There is only one Self shining through all. No one said it was easy at the offset. Yet, with a desire to play with people at this level of knowing, I found we could crack open the persona's need to judge and compare. That ego imp is always popping up to see how much pain it can inflict. If you cannot feel at peace with someone, then bless them and move on.

It was a practice for me. The magic came when I began to see how life flows when you need not react, close down or spend time thinking about who is worthy of your acceptance.

The outcome is extraordinary; the heart breathes more freely. The tension coming from judgment and resistance fades. The heart softens. The magic comes as you allow all to be as it is.

Woes of romantic love

My job as a master is to choose for eternity. It is to choose for peace. It is to choose for space and for a new angle of vision.

Long ago a man I loved left to be with someone else. My usual habit was to hate myself, hate the "gone away mate" and then find others who could be a chorus of woes with me.

It never worked. It never brought me peace. Now I knew a new way. So, this time? I sat up all night with the moon shining across the sky just feeling the raw sadness and the anguish run through me. Becoming present to all the threads of emotion as energy. I became the larger embrace and so saw them lose their power by morning. All night. In this? I let the fire burn through me. The fruits are many from that night.

Wonder Q: *Is love dependent upon another body being near me?*

No. Unless I choose it to be so. Do I wish to continue this belief? No. I want only freedom. If all is brought to me by my Holy Spirit, is this not a time to wonder and ask:

"What is the context of this event? What lesson am I learning here?"

For an entire night I breathed, cried, expressed, screamed and then, fell over. Yes, I gave up and accepted. I own no one; I give everyone the freedom to follow their own guidance.

In Presence and Allowing all

What I know full well is that the infinite Self cannot suffer, for it is the sky that embraces all that is. As I sit in Presence I allow all to be as it is. From this angle of vision, I see this flow of experience as that which has been called by me, for me. To bring me home.

Q: Does the persona/ ego self get bruised?
A: Yes. It was looking for something in the world to make it "happy" - love, fame, wealth.

Q: Who suffers? Who or what is it that knows this suffering? Knows the experience of joy? Knows all the different sensations and emotions which arise and pass away? What is it that remains and is always here and now?

What is it about you that does not change?

1. *I feel my way to the Soul.* Here is the challenge; once a feeling is allowed, felt, expressed and seen, the ego loses its power. Look even at the memories you carry of failure, of hurt and say, "Look at that. Yes I can feel that. Boy was I ever into that!" Shine the light of your awareness on it breathe with it. Extend forgiveness to yourself. And that shadow dissolves.

2. *Allowing all feelings* as I breathe. expressing them. Getting out of the head and into the heart.

3. *"If it is under my skin, it is mine."* No one is responsible for my experience except for me. As a sovereign soul I can choose in each moment how I wish to experience it.

4. *It is time to awaken from this dream of separation.* This belief in separation has become so habitual that most people do not question it. They go to dying in great fear. Yet, Heaven or nirvana is here and now. My attention has been with the dramas of the ego. And yet, you know how all melodramas end don't you? Now? "I am ready to be free."

5. *Arise up in your thinking.* Get the focus off of the small bit right in front of your nose and look up to the Light of higher consciousness."23

Silence is the threshold to the kingdom within.
After each breath, be still.
Let coming into the silence be a place you remember
often.
Relax the body, and the mind removes itself to a distance.
Release into the feeling-communion of the body.
Held within a cocoon of pure awareness you are safe.
You are permeated with this infinite awareness.

I call it home.

It is here, in this luminous stillness, that all is known.

Truth is one and absolute.

There is one animating cosmic spirit that flows through all that is arising. Whether you call it the Logos, God, the jewels of Indra, prana, Source, life force, Divine Mother, Alla'ha, Abba, Amma.

The names are many.

I talk with this indwelling spirit knowing it is my very best friend. Find your name for the infinite one. In truth? It is your very best friend, for it is your Self.

Stay present with whatever is arising.

As you relax into the breath of presence you begin to settle into the stillness. Inherent within you is a great peace.

Talk with this indwelling spirit knowing it is your spirit voice.

Yes, there are many perceptions in many humans; and yet?

Truth is One and is absolute.

All is perfect.

There is still the enchanted place in all of us, this sacred well, yet to tap.

You are being guided in each moment.
Your indwelling spirit calls to your self every event, every person, every wisdom teaching, every experience. You can then choose again. There comes a time where I was willing to let go of the dramas, let go of being a seeker and be the one who has found. Then? I chose to sit and be present.

I ask to remember my True Nature.

We continue to savor each experience, knowing it is what we all share. Knowing it is exactly what we have called to ourselves. And it is perfect. How can it be other?

The false self

The persona self (ego) is the false self.

"The reason you are so unhappy is that 99.99% of everything you do is for your self. And there isn't one."

- Wei Wu Wei

Ponder this and reflect on it. When I realized why people were as they were, I began to look into my own reactions, my own perceptions and my own beliefs. I was astounded. The world was simply my perceptions of it. It all took place in the mind.

Yes, the persona mind helps with conversation, planting tulips and remembering a dead aunt. This mind, when directed, also helps if you are writing letters or a term paper, writing anything and staying on the right side of the road.

Yet, it was never meant to be the master of your life. It is a servant of the awakened heart. At the core of your being is your True Self. When you tap into this you know the stillness that you are. Guidance follows. There is no more struggle.

Make your home in the Breath

Pondering:

In Reality the ego does not exist. It is the persona each of us creates, a tangle of memories, thoughts, beliefs, opinions, shame, guilt, fear and cultural and familial ideas.

Q: how do I outsmart the ego?

A: Never resist it. It is your creation. Play with it, get to know it's reactions, projections, judgements, confusions, doubts and deep feeling of lack. This knowledge takes away its power over you.

Remember the truth of who you are. Attune with Presence and say, "I am created as I was meant to be; perfect, innocent and eternal. I am an extension of the Infinite ONE. I am the presence of love in form."

Now: breathe the truth into the bones of your being. Then? Relax. I and my creator are one. I relax, I open to receive this peace....

this luminous and spacious Presence.

I become the huge embrace that is larger than these emotions.

I become the one who watches and allows.

I Am is the larger consciousness or the witness self. The perceiver.

The persona will say it is your duty to look upon every choice with seriousness. This is false, for your divine nature is one of joy. It is your birthright to know holiness and to remember, even in the activities of the world, who you are, and to go with a light heart; take yourself lightly.[24]

The persona mind is fear.
The ego is hell.
The ego is Satan.

Have we made this clear enough?

Fear

Fear comes from one insane belief, "I am separate from the Creator, the ground of all Being. I am alone, abandoned, a body that suffers and dies."

From this fear I bring attention to one teeny-tiny, itsy,bitsy part of my awareness and create an "ego." The dust on the dust of a wing of a gnat. That is how it sits within the unlimited and infinite cosmos of our beingness.

It is this persona, this mask of reactions and false perceptions that became the substitute for my own True Nature. My substitute in place of my divine, radiant being.

I come to believe in my own pretending.

I forget the truth from where I came forth.

No resistance.

Simply observe and embrace whatever is arising. love is allowing, embracing and trusting. Let it be as it is.

Begin to observe how the ego reacts and works in you, the images, judgements, beliefs and self-belittling thoughts it throws up;

Don't believe it.

Don't resist it for it simply gets more puffed up.

I talk with this ego persona, heres how it goes:

"Here's a familiar regret that I have at times, "You were supposed to be a concert pianist but got off track." Wow! Ms. ego you are so full of BS, let's just dance together.

There's that feeling of being sickly and not able to cope; I see you ego, yes, I do. That is such a lie!

"I feel unsupported and unloving." But, see here, you are the servant of this Soul that I am. No more running the show; I've got your number, I see how you work."

Explore it, Investigate it. Let it bathe in the warm bath of your consciousness; laugh at it. Yes, laugh at it. Yes, it is a clown with attitude and deserves to be in the sideshow of this life.

Tell it to be the servant of the heart.

Sit in Presence.

How did we make the ego?

As we identified with lack, fear and guilt there came about a very strong feeling of separateness, a feeling of abandonment. Along with this is a longing deep within, a feeling of homesickness, wanting to go home, a wanting to be held and nurtured, wanting to find that place of true love and acceptance, wanting to remember that which you are in truth. 25

A feeling of lack on all levels comes from this belief. No amount of money, not even a happy family can assuage the deep feeling of fear, lack, anxiety and despair.

And yet?

All along, our infinite consciousness, our true nature abides, waiting for us to turn our attention inward, to turn our attention to the truth; it is not about getting love. What I found is that you are a generator of love.

When we know this? We know Reality.

And realize the Truth of who we are.

Question: *how can therapy help?*

A: As a child I must first individuate and become a persona. Through psychology and the myriad of therapies today, I come to know my story. The belief in a "me" or an ego-self is reinforced. This is important for then I can see the threads of my personality, unresolved parental issues, those parts I dislike in myself. I see the obstacles to unconditional acceptance. Yet, if I begin to believe this ego exists in it's own right I lose myself in it's constant needs.

Through talk, drugs, memories, explanations, making art, journalling, and even dolphins, I feel better for being seen and heard. Telling my story is affirming. Coping with life is the outcome. Yet, as we know, it is short-lived. For it is not the truth of who you are.

Q: *What has been reinforced?*

A: The "me" that does not exist except as a conglomeration of my life's story. As long as we are propping up the ego without realization of the Soul we are in the land of falsehood and fantasy.

The antidote

Q: What now?

A: Sit and be with the emptiness, sit and be with the pain
that comes from old false programs, that comes from being both a
finite body and an infinite soul. Feel it entirely, all the old hurts
and wounds of existing in a complex family and in a world which
is, yes, insane. Where you were not seen as the perfection, the
innocent and shining one you truly are.

"No more whining."

Come into forgiveness and gratitude for this life, for the
earth, for all humanity and creation. It is rare to see this; Tibetan
monks, rishis, shamans, divine mothers and mystics are our
models. Yet, this allowing and trusting leads to a depth of
realization, of ultimate Reality, the truth we all share. This
illumination releases me from fear and misery and leads me to a
life of flow, ease and guidance.

Some people come into this naturally. Allowing your
creativity to flow through brings great delight. As you fall in love
with trusting and with allowing.

Whoever knows their Self, knows the Lord.[26]

What is it about me that does not change?
What is it about me that is continuous?
Feelings come and go. As do sensations and thoughts. Yet, this awareness of existing, does this come and go? I sit with this after a breath, feel into the spaciousness around me. Even the emptiness within.

As I give up believing in the world of dramas, as I give up living through the filter of the persona mind, as I relax, I realize this; God is not away in some heaven but permeates all of creation, both seen and unseen. Flowing through and around where I AM.

As I AM.
This I AM does not come or go. This realization of being alive. Of existing. This awareness of awareness.
Sit with this and know, right now, you are one with the ever-creating, ever-unchanged light which is love. There has never been separation.

We have a great God!

The Earth

"The old Lakota was wise. He knew that man's heart away from nature, becomes hard; he knew that lack of respect for growing, living things, soon led to lack of respect for humans too." [27]

What if there are millions of Christs, of Buddhas, of Medicine men, of shamans, of sufis and of awakened beings living from the heart, lightening up this earth? It is happening. Right now.

We are moving into a new era and with it we need a radical vision. Living from our fear-filled and false selves we have created chaos on this planet. Over billions of years she has developed and grown in companionship with indigenous cultures who learned from her secrets. Yet, in little over a century, with no reverence for all of life, we have put in jeopardy the world eco-system and ravaged this abundant, highly complex and giving planet. We have engendered life styles which decimate the land, the water and the very breath we breathe. [31]

"If we only knew deeply, absolutely, that our smallest act, our smallest thought has such far-reaching effects; setting forces in motion, reaching out to the galaxy; how carefully we would act and speak and think. How precious life would become in its integral wholeness." [28]

Listening within

Listening to nature

This year we noticed coltsfoot was springing up at various places on our land. We both had some breathing problems; what did we find? Coltsfoot has healing properties for the lungs. What plants are growing where you are in answer to your need or call? Constant dialogue is taking place. Are you listening? -EB

Throughout the world there is the tradition of direct perception of nature through the "intelligence of the heart ." Indigenous cultures share that their knowledge of plant medicine comes from the plants themselves and not through experimentation.

Discoveries in neuroscience prove that up to 25 percent of the heart is comprised of neural cells. The heart is, in truth, a brain in its own right. *The Secret Teachings of Plants,* Buhner,StephanHarrod

Heart-based perception is our birthright. It must be cultivated.

Who am I? What am I?

In Presence

I am pure consciousness.

I am stillness   I hear spirit in nature

I am love itself.

At the level of the persona or ego mind:

deep feeling of being separate and alone.

deep feeling of guilt

feelings of lack; lack of love, creative power, abundance,
     friends

feelings of greed, need, competitiveness, judgment,

feeling of anger and resentment

addiction to artichokes and movies

does not acknowledge others and puts others down.

feelings of being unseen. unloved, abandoned, criticized,
     judged, unloveable.

feeling of being unloved unloving.

wanting approval and wanting everything my own way.

wanting people to like me.

feeling full of rage yet acting nice.

fear of intimacy ingratitude arrogance

full of regret and full of wounds from the past.

full of anxiety about the future

full of regret meanness ingratitude

anxious about the future and suspicious

afraid of mice and snakes

mistrust of others.[29]

99

Troubled guest

I run from "uncomfortable feelings." Yet, it is those
uncomfortable feelings that are the roads to my real power. I sit
and let illness and mental suffering burn on. I talk to death and to
this ego so full of rage, so full of itself. I learn to accept. A good
thing I chose to remember this day in and day out. No resistance.
Breathe. Sit. Feel. Express.
Come into Presence.
Sit with a tree.

Self-realization cannot be found in words or directions.
Only in the recognition of oneness, of this ocean of pure
consciousness, pure beingness in which all arises, plays and
therefore? Father Sun Sister Moon, brother hills and sister plants,
we are one interwoven loving light family. As long as we live from
and through the heart.
This desire for deeper loving, for knowing this Infinite
GodSelf, this heart Self, I often fell into darkness. Even this kept
me searching.

....And so long as you haven't experienced
this: to die and so to grow,
you are only a troubled guest
on the dark earth.   Goethe

The Shaman sat with the woman who came with her sadness and depression, her feelings of loneliness and isolation. With great compassion he asked her:

"When was the last time you danced?
When was the last time you sang?
When was the last time you told a story to a friend?"

When did you sit
with the plants and
listen? When did
you feel into the
emptiness and ask:
who is it that suffers?

Authentic in each moment

An intense feeling is a call to allow, feel, express.
move with it. At a certain point I simply sit and let it move
throughout my being. I breathe into it. I sit.

It is a call to pay attention. Then, I can choose to
sit and let the feeling play through the nervous system.
fear is a thread of energy that needs to be allowed.

The suffering comes when I resist it.

It is the resistance that causes suffering, not the feeling
itself.

Sit with it. Feel how it moves around in the body.

Notice how good you feel after crying, expressing your
fear or anger, telling your truth to a friend and being authentic in
each moment.

Make your home in the breath

*Each of us chooses our own chariot. For me it was Horse and
the bus. As a child I rode buses from one grandmother to another.
And then, I learned to conjure and ride the cosmic horse. One thing?
Arriving at the gate may be less thrilling than the ride itself. -
Milwaukee, 1956.*

Our indwelling spirit uses all our creations to bring us
home. Chariots: Which do you choose for this mysterious and
forever life? Who has brought you a new vision or changed the
direction of your life?

My chosen home, growing up, was a number of stables
owned by people eeking out a living on the falling down edges
of suburbs and cities. My father was looking for that pot of gold
over the next hill. Always somewhere else. So we left the south
and its humid embrace and headed north. On the Silver King
Railroad we left New York state, and headed for Wisconsin. In
Milwaukee he traded our house for another unseen in California,
so we went back to the west. My father knew how to
orchestrate a trip with tales of great celebrities, with movies
once disallowed. Yes, and then he said, "Zane Gray lives above
us." Seems he was hidden in Yucca plants and on an
impassable trail where I would sit in the early mornings, and
sing. Singing old Irish songs, "Oh, you are a mucky kid. Dirty
as a dust pin lid...." like the night-sky, brought me out of the
kerfuffle of family and into myself.

Every year and a half or so we had a new house
somewhere in a state with names like Wisconsin, California,
Maryland, New York, names I repeated over and over in dark
rooms, feeling how they felt in the mouth. All beautiful sounds
with amoebic shapes on maps stained with my father's fears,

longings and the truly American desire, "to be someone." While tucked within these shapes, waiting to be discovered, were winding rivers, forests, glacial lakes and strange animals with horns. On my tongue the sounds of them left a sweet citrus tang. Nights were spent hanging on the window sill and swimming in the night sky. And, as always, as we began a new foray, bubbling over with anticipation.

For there are the dreams of riding all out and lightning hot over the prairies and up mountains and through rivers which keep me nourished for years to come. Fed by Zane Gray, Black Beauty, Walter Farley, Hopalong Cassidy, Annie Oakley and the Lone Ranger, there was more than just the thrill there. Hidden even from me was the soul message, vague yet always pressing through; don't get stuck. Don't be confined. Stay alert. You can ride off into the sunset. At anytime.

This yearning to escape comes on the wings of many events; sickness and so much time alone. Whispers about my heart and its funny murmur. So then, let's ride out with the cowgirls, ride out in style, escape often and pay attention to these desires, this yearning. For in the seeds of desire? I found my passion and glory and a few keys to some hidden rooms in my psyche. Without countless projects, singing alone in my room, without these breaks from life in a house, in a bed, from a life that may crush your yearnings, from a life in a frail body, without these endless creations there is a shrinking back. There is fear. And a gnawing for a freedom, which seems to be veiled and only partially seen, on the other side of the mountain. The unmet teacher. The foggy barely pencilled in somewhere else.

In the meantime. ....

Horse called to me. Horse can carry you away. Horse is unpredictable. Horse listens; she knows you from your fears right down to your boot size. You cannot pretend with horse.

Some barns were run by small Napoleonesque men with booming voices on large, anxious horses. Some by women who lived and loved together between the highways and the meadows of gold corn and cottonwoods. Some were run by small families with huge hayfields. For me? Their names and those summers all finally ran downstream into one hammering and terrifying syllable: Mac.

*

In Wisconsin during the summers I spend every Saturday at this sprawling stable called Joy Farm. Owned by a Swedish man with huge arms, a voice that curdles the blood, a barrel chest and wildly gesturing silver blonde hair; it is a riding place for 8-18 year olds.

Mac is king and judge and runs the barn with his crop cocked skyward as his jaw follows. Built for action, he is a man of commands and questions. In the ring he rubs this crop along the steel rafter, sounds that crack the eardrum, frighten horse into a panic and send me spinning.

"I do this," he said, "to teach you riders something about balance. More than that? This is how the game can change in a blink." A huge whack to the rafter and the circle is set in motion.

The game can change in a blink; do I take that one in? A thousand times a hundred times. Yes.

Mac whacks you on the thigh when you deviate from the righteous circle. It is the circle which will enter into my days and my dreams as I recall the balancing on this whirlwind called

Horse. With at least a hundred horses, as many acres of trails and the chance to ride in the parade on the fourth of July, these tired barns hold us in our charged expectations and tight jodhpurs. We are proud in our uniforms of leather boots, hard hats and tiny crops. Tough kids all waiting for Horse and, oh, the parade!

What is this America, this world, without parades? What is childhood here without parades? Unimpressed by ball sports, except baseball, throughout the year I willed myself to put up winter, with frozen eyes and numb toes, withstanding it all because it was prologue and led right into the fourth of July. It led to that bright pathway to paradise; the parade.

*

To get there and to share in this freedom ride? I have to take a bus. The bus swerves through cornfields and past farm houses with wood stacked high, cows and pastures sloping green and furrowed far into the sky. Cows and more cows sleepy, grazing. Even the clouds had horns and tails and milky colors.

In the back of the bus sit the older girls. At seventeen they talk of things left unspoken. They are horsewomen with attitudes that run from outrage to giggles to awe to intense quiet. Marlboro cigarettes are lit up, coca colas brought out from brown bags and for the next hour I am a garden of ears. They talk about boys, sex, feelings, horses, Jesus (JEEEEESUS and GAWD whose names never came to our table at home), teachers and nuns. The bus is a world of the unexpected.

There is Sheila with a fat auburn pony tail and the biggest reddest mouth I have ever seen. Her jeans hug a body so sensual it might burst through the seams of her jeans and propriety at any moment. Tough and cool she smokes and chews gum at the same time. It was a Oscar winning attitude this shakti goddess in flannel and denim.

And there is Kathy. She is also tall and slender; she is a cowgirl Elizabeth Taylor without make-up. It is Kathy whose presence makes me sit up straight. When she speaks I listen.

A pause here for I realize that Kathy, more than the others, set up a room in the theater of this mindscape right from day one. She held me. Throughout my life she has returned as if we had set a series of dates in which to talk, once again, and share the questions and the longings that life presents.

Why, I ask? Kathy owned two horses and went to a Catholic high school. Back then, I pictured her in movies kissing her boyfriend endlessly. Something in her manner claimed my attention; was it perseverance or grace? Partially those. Yet, why did she not let me go? What kept me tuned into her every word and every move? Unspoken the feeling was, "If I grow up I want to be like her."

In the ring, once we smaller riders come down from the unstoppable circles, Kathy is sailing her horse B. Barrymore over small jumps. Graceful even as she is flying off onto the ground, and on again, and over again and again until they are a team. Away from the others Kathy is surrounded by an implacable peace. She exudes a calm, which might have been taken for sadness, that emanates from her very skin. That is it, a peace which I had never seen before.

There was a boy on the bus. To be sure, he was more of a trickster; his name was Eli. Blonde, quiet and with a grin and a "hi" for us little kids, he was the cowboy who came into this cast of characters without fanfare. Once at the farm, Eli could be

107

seen riding his horse, a palomino, upside down, head to saddle, feet in the air, as he whispered her into a rocking canter. Yes, an upside down headstand in the saddle while she canters in circles to his voice commands.

Extraordinary. Amazing it seemed to me that this somewhat awkward kid could become graceful as serpents and wind himself everywhere on that horse. Eli was a trick rider; I think of him now as a warrior. In the movies only the Native Americans rode as if they were part of the horse. For he was no mortal but was cousin to a centaur and the son of shape shifters.

I waited for his hellos as I waited for him to lift me up on Little Girl; he never did. A first yearning. He offered me that mixture of fear, excitement and a tingling in my face. The blood blushes me and takes off into the wilds of secret passions, fantasies and vaguely seen enactments. He was my first brush with the enigma of passion. Dancing with this gentle boy and horse and now, this too, to the child was a new possibility.

Also on the bus were two friends around my age; one was Tasha who loved books, playing jacks and horses, and felt that being ten was an achievement. The other was Carrie who is also in fourth grade. Her fate was in her lovely red hair and her enormous chest. She rides horses who move easily from a walk to a canter. Trotting jars and plays havoc with those over-large breasts so her mother had a bra specially made for her, size D. On horseback her soft moans (oooh, eee, ayahhhh) alert me that she is trotting.

Alarmed by Carrie I have an inspiration. One Friday night, alone and in the tub, I pray and pray that I will remain flat as a board so I can ride any horse forever. This may be a test to

108

see whether the universe listens and if God has my best intentions in mind. It feels like a real asking. A year later? Three years later? My prayers are answered in my bodily truth. Eureka.

In reality, nothing rallies on my chest until I am around twenty four years old and that is minimal. But something inside of me had lit up. Asking. Maybe asking is a key. I knew nothing of the bible or the Sufis, "Ask and you shall receive. Knock on the door, leave yourself outside and come in." Backing into asking is another way, for some, as it was for me then; and the desire to control this quirky, elusive, yet, very real body and overwrought mind.

Barely conscious of what this baptism of water and the initiation of asking means, I keep it held close in my heart. So many secrets already flapping around in that house, another might sail it right off its foundation. The feeling of being heard stayed with me. Happy with my skinny chest and delighted still with my rubber duck who swims and can never be drowned, I am content.

Never for too long though, for as soon as the bus arrives Mac crashes, with no hellos or how are ya's, into our world, "Get those horses tacked. Five minutes to show time." Then the fear and the excitement become one as we who choose the way of Horse, are propelled into that ring of circling, circling, circling. Nothing up ahead but back around again and again.

It ignited some hidden blueprint of the journey of the absurd. The now here and nowhere to get to place. Mac yells it out, "Mind those stirrups, toes up, heels down." Balance, yes, for you knew what happened if you lost a stirrup, the long slide out of the circle and the quest for union, a quest for giving up control and bowing to the unpredictable, wild and wily spirit of Horse.

Then? I only knew I felt grand on Horse. For those who wanted ribbons it was a passion and a heartbreak; for those looking for freedom it is an ever deepening intimacy with the purity of nature. Horse shares her spirit, and keeps calling me back to myself. "Be here with the trees, the mountain and the birds. Be here with me." No pretensions, she honors her word to be true to herself. Always, as incandescent and mysterious as a waterfall, never holding back, unable to be false, so off on a whim and a hearty "Gettup."

For me? I learn to ride and I learn to fall. I want to be with birds and forests and to lie in the emerald grass as Horse grazes near me. I want to feel the pulse of earth and the dome of sky and to rest. Finally, yes, to rest. At the end of the ride. Knowing full well that it can all change in a blink.

*

In that cast of riders was a cast of characters from the theater of this life which I continue to meet; the intellectual, the warrior, the contemplative, the trickster, the teacher, the wild woman, the artist, the mother, the lover, and me, the watcher. Beneath the appearances and the roles we play is the Infinite Self holding us as gently as the sky holds a cloud. Bubbles in the expanse of the infinite.

To be continued

Say "yes" to all that is arising in this moment. Say Yes, to the unknown. Say Yes to not-knowing.

When you say "Yes" you attune yourself with the glory and the power of the moment. Now. And to the infinite. This is the only true gift you can give to the world, your Presence, rooted in your beingness. This realization allows you to see the perfection through the dramas and the kerfuffles that seem to run the world.

Yes yes yes yes yes yes yes yes yes

Yes to Reality. Whatever is happening, it is perfect. No mistakes and nothing is wrong. Yes to the unknown and to all that arises

Do you see?

Soul School

This I know full well, that each being, each soul comes to earth to experience and learn and grow from its own "vision quest." Coming from a number of lives it has it's own agenda.

I take power away from another by seeing him/her as a victim of the world. There are no victims here, there are only sovereign souls.

I give back power when I see her/him as a soul-invincible, indestructible, perfect and free.

From this place we walk out of victimhood into mastery.

It is time to wake up from this dream.

There is conflict in being alive, in a body with thoughts that arise and fall away, of ideas, beliefs, memories, yet nothing to hang onto in this little mind.

There is conflict and there is pain, pain from our realization of our own feeling of lack. Pain is the hawk, the messenger. While the message is, okay, listen to this, turn within, it is time to wake up.

Wanting to fix this feeling of emptiness I go to a therapist. Instead of sitting and experiencing the feeling associated with life in the body. Instead of simply stopping everything and allowing the feelings, I look for a fix.

The way-showers from all paths say the same thing; there is nothing to fix, it is time to wake up. It is time to embrace all that is arising - and see what comes from this. What I have learned? The way out is the way through. The way through is feeling all feelings to their roots with no resistance. acceptance, allowance, trust.

*If you breathe in and are aware that you are alive
then you can touch the miracle of being alive - then that is a
kind of enlightenment. [30]*

After two years on the bus, I climb into my usual place in the back with Tasha and Carrie. We keep on rolling past Kathy's stop as if she is not there. She must be here. Her empty space next to Sheila jars my sense of balance. The tribe has shrunk. Tasha and I lapse into a silence.

After the "where is she?" question, after pauses and eye rolls, Sheila's voice explodes.

"Kathy said no to everything," she blurts as we roll on, sewn together in her smoke and the abrupt snorts of her teen rage.

"She's eighteen," Sheila goes on, "What do any of us know? She said no to college. No to the horses. She said no to Michael her boyfriend." (No? No? No to kissing him forever through the nights of my mind making? Are you joking me? My mind stutters). And no to riding over hills and beyond the trails that we longed for; to that world out there which glows and calls with it's secret promises of some things wonderful and never before seen.

"She took herself away." Sheila drops her ash. She hangs the words above us. A broad gap as Sheila collects herself, blows a smoke ring. "She said 'yes' to a vow of silence for seven years."

A yawning gap. Then, a pause.

"She's in a convent. Kathy became a nun."

Foreign words spat out and the world goes a-kilter. A door inside of me closes shut. For here it was; Kathy had not fallen off the bus into illness, no, for that would have been acceptable. No, she had taken herself off and was never, ever, coming back. Ever, ever, never. That never word.

What sat in my craw like lead was this; she hadn't come to say good-bye. She, along with a beloved Uncle Hank and Big Daddy my grandfather, and a number of animals, left without a "good-bye" and my heart was shredded. Abrupt leavings. A sour off-key wang to the heart valves.

In this life I call mine, there manifested an anxiety around sudden exits. Not conscious as to the why, I found ways to orchestrate good-byes even after a dinner or a party. For it might mean a forever good-bye. Without a good-bye how would I know the love we shared, how would they know I cared or that I was still in their world?

On the bus I looked out the window, tears steaming and an internal cry on the edge of a shriek, then swallowed. Only Tasha looked at me, her marble gray eyes flecked with questions. We swam together silently in our pond of betrayal. For us Kathy had not looked back. As kids we feel each look, each word as a fullness of the light of being seen. Kathy had taken back the light.

Did joy continue on the bus? Joy had a lobotomy, or at least a face lift. For Kathy and her horses, her beauty and grace, were now just a memory. Even the clouds were tangled and snarly and blanking out the sun.

That way she could fall onto the dried manure floor of the arena and as she arose, still be fresh and unscathed, Athena from the head of Zeus, that way was no more. All gone in the flick of Sheila's pissed off smokelets, as they curled into nothingness before our eyes.

115

Riding through the mind-garden, sunlight is streaking onto the cornfield. Birds in an autumn swooping and the sky more blue than Cellini's. Tall in the saddle, she sits. Bobbing above the fields, riding with straight back and long black hair, B. Barrymore's flared nostrils and thick mane. Trotting in spirals, outward from the ever moving geometry and kaleidoscope I call memory. Is truth here in this mindscape? Shall I write of my dreams and all these loose curls and phantom fantasies we call memory?

She is Centauress, Diana, Isis, Athena and St. Clare all rolled into one; she is this tribe of Goddesses who pulls me onto her horse. "Come," they say, "We want to show you something." I am behind her holding on. Beneath us, this trusty chariot pushing us up with dynamo hind legs as he reaches flat-out to carry us over fences, over streams, over Mr. Swanson's chicken coop he flies, one brook gone, then another, all gone, gone again. I am clinging tightly to her waist, barely holding on.

B. Barrymore floats us over the trails right up to the door of the stoney convent where Kathy dismounts. We are breathing hard together, B. Barrymore and I. Kathy knocks a tepid knock. Now, bolder, a real cowgirl knock. Horse fidgets with the bit; the door opens inward and as she steps, her stirrups clacking on stone, inside where we dare not follow, I ask for the meaning of it all. She smiles.

What then? She disappears into a dark cavern. A place of darkness and deprivation? A place of whispers and hope? Horse neighs and a herd appears. Even in a nunnery the wild horses will come to get you, if you ask. Kathy is not reluctant and does not turn back. No good-bye. Just her stirrups clanking on the stones. And then? Just the silence.

Silence.

*

Whacked in the heart. Shut down. Hurt and pain. The heart of the child is always wide open. I can pretend to close it up. The mind is that strong. If I keep on pretending I will be catatonic in a corner, curled up, barely breathing. The gesture of shrinking back and away from life for fear of being broken kept me fragmented and wary. Until I met those who reached out and said, "no more. There is a way out of this fear, this pain."

*

To live in this heart, I must not shut down. I must allow the rawest of feelings to sweep through me. This fearlessness is part of trusting spirit. I came to know this; so I let it be purged in the roughest of waters through its soft canals, I let it be broken open, burned through, sloshed and fed with whatever miseries and guilts move in this field of life; with raw anger I let it marinate. Allow. Embrace what arises. Guilt or shame, fear or sense of lack. Bring it on.

Remember this, it is not personal. Soon it all boils down into tributaries of feelings moving through all my brothers and sisters everywhere. We are the same. I realized how the earth, the trees and animals along with the mountains help to transform and hold all that we offer up; all the anger and the wonder.

There is no sin or need for salvation; but there is a need to feel completely and know that grace travels within the waters of these rivers. I know all kindred spirits have been so broiled and cooked up, and then? This unforeseen opening follows.

Grace, some call it.

Life on the planet is contrast and the unknown. Live in the unknown and you will know the Infinite dearly. Build walls and make rigid protective armors, you are sure to be led through even more devastating terrain. You may be led through those events which vibrate and slam at the rigid barriers built to keep feelings, love, intimacy and people at bay. Illness. Divorce. Accidents, all may follow. Will follow. All to bring us home.

Yet, here is the rub; our feelings are the surest way to incarnate fully; being authentic makes us real. It takes a bravery. It takes a deep desire to grow. Sometimes? To die to what was the self. And then? To grow.

Back to the bus:

" What do you do in a convent?" Tasha ventures quietly.

"You talk with God." Sheila bursts out. "Oh, and you take care of people. Poor people."

My insides are flopping along with the bouncing wheels, the bus driver still in place, but all of it now tilted, yes, no longer on a page I can turn to. Having no ideas, nothing to hang onto the "convent" word there is a lull in the trustworthy ride. Given Sheila's disdain, I knew it must be a place where cigarettes, gum, red lipstick, Jeesus jokes and horses were not in abundance. A prison? No. She rode there on her own. Maybe. But who knows?

A vague and shifting worry begins to uncurl it's serpent smile. A place in which old women in strange headresses with robes that whisper as they walk intone your name and you disappear. With no parades and no kids. And most probably? No peanut butter and jelly sandwiches. The mind maze serves up disasters.

"Kathy left the world to serve God." Sheila is done. It is a mind loop.

*

Show me this God, I say to her. Introduce us. Sometimes late at night, I ask her, "Was it worth it? Do you not miss this life of being carried by bus and horse, of dates and movies, of dancing all night until you fall down, of trotting through cottonwoods, your whole body on fire with the smells of pine, lily of the valley and the musk of horse?"

Her face is still and she's listening.

Now I say, "The ride, in the snow, with the wind uprooting your hair, whirling you into whipped cream; you know it better than most, the ride is beyond all else on this planet." Riding together with the sky, hills, trees and hawks, something so beyond words, is this not God?

Perhaps it is like a canary suddenly given her freedom from a cage of house or school.

"Kathy, do you not see it?" Now the frantic feeling in the throat and chest, the feeling just before tears come. I can humiliate myself with a deep weeping, nose crapping, eyes swelling into a sobbing into a howling so beyond crying it brings me to my knees. How can you live without knowing how it will turn out? Your kids faces? And all those kids on, downward into eternity?

Smug me. There is this edge to my inner voice. Yet, I continue to hold little mind meetings in which I corner her and make her fess up. Sometimes we share a hot chocolate. I want her to speak. Cry with me? Probably not. I want to know why? Did you go out of fear? Did Jesus call you? Are there nun police who come in the middle of the night? I want answers.

She sits as if she is always and still on her horse, straight and removed from my questions. Detached. She is unseeing of my sticky fingers as I spill my chocolate over the table. The edge turns into a knife; I want to see her react. Beg for a way out. Change your mind. There is still time. Please be kidding.

Later, older, more knowing in the way of the world's antics I tell her how the cosmic light filters through his exquisite breath; how the heart is taken right away, how it goes on expanding to take in this grand and fiery love, all of nature, this love in a fiery jacket, called God-Horse. Horse inhales as you exhale; for now it can be said, horse is the cosmic horse as well as the supple bone and blood horse beneath you.

120

Kathy, how could you leave us? I miss knowing you still. I miss knowing your answers to all the secrets about God and the universe; and me. (What I mean to say, truly is; who needs heaven when paradise is this garden, right here, made for hooves and horse breath and young men's kisses in forever nights?)

The earth offered so much as I spent days outside in meadows or sitting on Horse while he grazed. Breathing wind.

Then, as I graduate from high school, feeling the full swell and ebb of my own sensuality while diving deeper into literature and biology, I know Kathy better. I have crawled into her age you see, into some of her desires, and on the bus of life I have status. For isn't that what we are looking for? As our roads diverge further, still I feel this kinship call me.

A few more conversations come and go.

So I try getting to the nub of the thing; the question arises, forget the fun and laughter, what about freedom? Look, I am free to drink wine, try Maryjane and be with whoever I wish, free to ride the bus with Ken Kesey. Why, I am free to go anywhere at anytime, have a baby or no, ice cream in forty flavors, and make love with whomever. America, after all, is a wonder of freedoms.

She is quiet. "You will know very soon what the world can give you. Here", she says, "I am free. Here I have the entire universe." She points to her heart and the smile upon her lips is as knowing as Simone Signoret or Sister Corita. She has fallen into a calming prayer. Seven years' silence turns into fifteen. Still she twinkles in the matrix field of my being.

—EB

Pondering

Most people are lost in their experiences - thoughts, feelings, perceptions sensations and relationships. Most people seek fulfillment through these forms. This always brings suffering. See the life around you as a film. There are colors, shadows, lights and movement on a screen/field of consciousness which is ever the same. It is like the screen of a movie.

Is the screen changed by the flow of cars, houses, trees, people that move across it? If there is a fire does the screen burn? If there is a rainstorm does the screen get wet? The unreality of the moving images is much like the unreality of this world of forms. Yet, all forms whether thoughts, houses, sensations, perceptions, all must have a medium, a 'screen' upon which to be experienced. A field which allows all to arise and pass away.

Ponder this.

To transform the mind, claim the truth:

"My presence is a blessing to all creation."

This is the truth. If you don't know this, then, please, use time to truly take it in, play with it, dance with it, grok it. Give up the dance of smallness, the dance of the victim and the dance of the little self (which has never existed). Notice if old conversations arise. See the patterns. Embrace it. Notice.

Then exult. In however you exult. find your way to exult.

EXULT   EXULT   EXULT!

Inner Sanctums

It is not enough for a person to know how to ride;
she must know how to fall.   -Mexican
Proverb

Kathy saw her need for quiet and a structured life. She was not swayed by the culture of more, the culture of materialism. She listened to her heart deeply. She, I believe, loved this invisible Lord, this mystery of existence. I asked, what took you there? Was it the fantasy of a man-savior who would come and take you into some paradise? Yes, she said as a finale to my questions. "Masters are everywhere, but the world does not see them."

She was my double, my sister in exile. Or was I the one in exile? And this was the nub of it; in my life, then, what was more exciting than singing, the pull and flare of the horse beneath you, the promise of loving a beautiful boy, the swirl in a new skirt? Happiness came in from the world; this seemed obvious. Then.

Was it not possible to live in the world and still know the Infinite One? I was unsure. Courage and strength is all it takes. Maybe.

Later, I took to finding quiet and to reading St. Theresa of Avila, St. Augustine, Ramakrishna, William Faulkner and Thomas Merton. Biblical phrases returned to ignite Yogananda's reason for coming to the west; that at the core of all spiritual traditions is the one truth. God is "the one in whom we live, move, and have our being" (Acts 17:28). And always riding through forests and along rivers and knowing where to see the sun coming up and the moon going down.

Life went on with friends, teaching, writing, singing. Songs came through or not. Later, I would follow her into those sanctums to find a peace without conditions. But then? I felt I was missing something, some teacher or some visionary. I wanted a master teacher. I wanted certainty. So I went on, threading together experiences and living as if the secret of life and death was out there, in the world and coming to my theater soon.

Curiosity about Jesus, about the masters of India and the middle east, about Kathy, about those who took themselves away from the world, arose and fell back. This felt a conflict in my core. The skirting the edges of the mystic life and the wanting to be someone; this wanting to prove to my father I was strong. But, truly, who and what and where? Art pulled as did graduate school. Yet, fame and fortune did not pull me. When he listened to my songs his only question is: "Are they on the radio yet?" Not yet. Not yet.

*

Eighteen years after her leaving, and on a short visit to the midwest, I run into A., who, as a child, bought Kathy's horse. I had stopped for food in a foreign part of Milwaukee and there she was with her mother in a grocery store. Pondering now on the mazes and twists my spirit went through to bring us together, I asked them, once more, "Is Kathy still a nun?"

"Yes," they answer, "she is still at the same monastery. She is still in silence." Only one thing I wanted to ask Kathy, "Did God call you? And, please, answer me this, did he call you by your name?"

*

125

Time seemed to pass. College over and I spent years recovering from hepatitis. Instead of following a plan for graduate school in art, I was dealing with a body both weak and yellow and weighing in at 75 pounds. Once able, I set out to be somewhere else. Anywhere. I healed and set off for Oregon.

As I rise up and look at this life, as if I am a raven high above the earth looking at this moving pattern of life, here is what I see. While I was otherwise involved I was sent a car crash, a flood in Florence, Italy, a volcano in Oregon, a bombing while in Bali and many others, saying; "You think this world is safe? Really? You believe it can give you something of value?" Look here. As tsunamis come and go, as glaciers melt, as friends leave their bodies, the epiphany dawns; I am not in control. This world we have created as a substitute for the truth of the Infinite is unsafe and is not our true home.

Once back in New England, finally, after years of living on the fringe and dipping my toes into this world, after years of riding the same little mare up apple orchards, over streams and through the hills of New England, I would want, finally, would look, rigorously, for those places in which there is, yes, silence. Forests, ashrams, convents, Yoga retreats, Buddhist retreats, pilgrimages, Way of Mastery retreats, Goddess dancing and finally a cottage alone on a pond in western Massachusetts.

Lovers appear, songs are caught and composed from the fragments given me in silence or in turmoil, friends share meals and there is much laughter, dancing and music always, living in the world. But alone and in silence I see myself half-baked. Swimming and sitting in a dell in a forest. In between the screaming world and my own demons and cares, there is the silence.

I could not live in a world where there was no meaning except to accrue more ideas and money, more social events and social approval. In nature I felt the awe and wonder of something present. Something within was calling.

"Worlds may crash around you, meteors may collide, but you know you are safe as you are one with the Infinite One who birthed you." [31]

I joined Kathy finally in that place of silence, the place of stillness she was, I believe now, always riding towards, whether on Horse, on the bus or in a convent. And I waited.

*

Speak only if it improves upon the silence. [32]

One spring day, in a Los Angeles bookstore, an orange volume shone from among many; *Autobiography of a Yogi* by Paramahansa Yogananda. The language of it held India's sweetness, flowery language and the bliss of enlightenment. All new to me then, this book is now a classic, translated into all the world languages.

In 1925 he established an international center for Self-Realization Fellowship in California, which became the spiritual and administrative heart of his growing work. Lights went off; I felt I had found a teacher in answer to something buried deep within me. I discovered that Yogananda was the first Hindu teacher of yoga to spend a major portion of his life in America.

I notice something immediately; in all the pictures of this lineage of saints, right in the middle is Jesus, the Mystic Christ. Yes, I had left the Baptists and the Presbyterians behind;

but there was always this wonder question, who was Jesus truly? What did he teach really? Yogananda saw Jesus as an incredible master of consciousness - of Love.

The core of Jesus message was the same as Yogananda's; remember your oneness with the Infinite; God consciousness. As a member of his Self-Realization Fellowship I met Bob Raymer, a great friend of Yogananda; a true master and teacher. Along with new friends met through the center we began to breathe and sit together, walk and reflect.

Yogananda asked only one thing of his friends; develop the discipline of breath and meditation for two hours a day for a year. Then, see if you know the peace of the infinite. Without this observing the mind, this breathing and the silence, it is all trivial talk. For truth and Reality, he wrote, are within.

Ah, a challenge. My favorite. I took him up on this. Then, I saw everything as a challenge. "The word 'discipline'," he said, " means to be a disciple of truth." And, "remember, " Yogananda wrote. "There is nothing to get from this world, for it is a deception. The seed of the Infinite is within you. "

Often now, I join Kathy in this inner temple of silence and sit as the twilight comes on and we turn night into day. All mystics are exactly alike in this dive out of the world. Yet, the world is innocent. I came to accept my life, accept it all as exactly right. I do not need to be a nun or a Buddhist or a Christian or any other label. I simply accept that who I AM is all that is.

*

I still ride the bus from nowhere to somewhere and back again to now-here. I still love the rollicking ride on horse where everything merges into an everywhere at once - bus, babies crying, apples shining, orchards, orange lips, centaurs, songs arising, root beer floats, horses flying, and the hair of the corn glowing from a sun which blesses all alike. The sound of the wheels turning soothes.

So, what is there to do but sit back and relax? Pass the paper bags, be wondrous at the birdsong, and give yourself up to this ride. All dramas end the same: There will be the last station on the last bus and this we know full well. Till then? Notice the other passengers, help them on, help them off. Be grateful for this life, for it is a gift.

All rides on all chariots, including this earth on its circling galactic tour, finally bring what you came to learn. If your desire is to awaken from the dream, and melt into your Essence, then the end is perfectly certain.   Bare Hill Pond, Ma. 1991

… consider the world as a temporary stop, a little longer one. We all are traveling, and this is yet another place we are visiting. So, the moment you meet a person or settle in a place, maintain awareness that someday you will have to part.[33]

Pondering:

There are no mistakes and nothing is without purpose.

Somehow, somewhere you believe you have failed, and because of that many feel they cannot awaken. As you begin to feel some joy, there will be the message, "No, no I cannot feel that much joy." And you begin to contract the heart yet again because it is a pattern learned in the mind. It feels like you because you are used to it. It is familiar.

That is how the dream of separation becomes comfortable. Yet? It is an illusion of the mind. As you breathe the light in, as you claim the truth, not the ego's falseness, you remember.

Nothing is random. Holy spirit uses all your creations-events, accidents, illnesses, people, books, films, regrets and yes, even your rages to help you remember your true Self.

Think of three people in this life who changed you in some way.

Who was it that loved you without conditions? How did that feel?

Who stopped you in your tracks, caught your attention, and in some way called you to stop and listen?

And remember, was there someone or some event that changed the direction of your life?

The mystery - a reminder

Existence is an utter mystery that no one—not the greatest of philosophers nor the greatest of mystics has ever or will ever comprehend.
No one.
Not ever.
It is not a problem to be solved but a moment to be lived.
Played in and enjoyed
It is given.
It is a gift.
Not for anything I have done but simply because the
Creator's desire is to manifest Love.
All creation is an extension of THAT.
You are an extension of THAT.

Every loving creation is eternal and every loving thought is true.
The Creator is but Love and Love can only begat Love.

At the end of the road, at the end of a marriage,
 is a trail into the unknown.
Take my hand and lets follow the swallowtail.
She seems to know her way through.   -EB

Divorce. A two year marriage that never was. I asked for annulment, he said, "please no." I left letters on the sofa, on the pillows, on the kitchen counter, pushing my loneliness and sadness into his world that he might turn and look at me.

So I left with these words: "If you want to go to a counselor with me, I hold that space open for six months. After that? I will take it that we are no longer married."

Now, wherever I went, a shadowy being walked with me, ate at my table and hovered over my bed. She came as a bellyache in my heart. Shame, and then, her sister guilt dallied with my fears and dreams. I had left a marriage and taken from it only what I had brought with me: five thousand dollars, a yellow lamp and a salamander called "Trust" still resting in my pocket. He is a gift from my Uncle Hank who said, "Bits, you must smoke a corncob pipe. And you must alway carry a fierce but gentle lizard in your pocket. His name is Trust. No matter what the world brings you."

I left behind an airy belief that marriage, a mate and a house would bring happiness. Now? As I hiked the Cascades of Oregon, the vow of aloneness was my mantra. Inside? I felt lost and unable. I belonged nowhere. I had no idea what the future would bring; but I would not die feeling alone while living with a made up someone who could not share or take my hand. We left each other to find new trails.

Oregon was the fertile and wild green Goddess I had been told about; her mountains rising to the clouds motioning me to look up. Some of my days spent without agenda of any kind, simply roaming through meadows rife with flowers so new to the eye. There were Indian paintbrush, lilies and trillium, India pipe and wild mushrooms and all glowed back from this wet and mossy forest bed.

Here I see my first black bear, close up. Here, rafting on rivers winding through country both wild and petal soft I heard them calling out, "Come, bathe here, come sit and let the wind freshen your spirit, console your heart and bring on the deepest sleep found on this earth." I breathed in the purest air from the highest peaks over lakes that shone out luminous in the waves and waves of mountains. The earth, now a refuge and a glory, became my mate, my food, my balm. I slept on her beds and drank from her brooks.

What was I looking for? A place to sing into the nights? A place to feel a part of something grander? Freedom was something new to me. I found out that to feel truly free is to be at home sleeping in the foothills or in an upland meadow and to wash your face in a mountain stream.

I have seen gothic cathedrals and even, in Barcelona, Gaudi's La Sagrada Famiglia; yet, all fall short of walking out into a forest, a meadow, a lake in this still untrammeled Oregon. Without the bone shucking winters of the northeast, the ocean called even in January. The flower saints of John Muir, along with the mountain temples, the clouds rampaging through, all gathered into this playing field of the Lord and calling out to me like a long-lost and loving Sister. Mount

133

Hood rose above the city of Portland and was a compass for all our days.

A year passes and the marriage that never was is now a memory. I am abiding with the lostness and the failure of all the expectations and brilliant images I had of 'marriage.'

I take some painting classes at PSU. I will get an MFA. Near the campus is a small place called the Questing Beast Tavern; it has a legend around it. Street poets and loggers with essays hold forth some nights. Always live music. Everyone is welcome here. I am curious. One day I take my guitar, a few lumps in my throat and shuttle up to the doorway to push lightly. Barely open I stand, the old meekness running me into that woefully unprepared stance, not completely in or out of the door. I gaze inside; the smell of whiskey wilts my will.

Widening, the darkness pulling my eyes out to a man moving fish-like through the place, talking and joking and staving off a perturbed but lovely bartender. The sound "WOMAN" blares from her presence as she wipes down the maple wood bar surface. Full bodied with blonde hair traipsing down her back, amber eyes that never leave the fisher king who is, now, on his way towards me and now, right before me. Long silver flecked hair, a bandanna Willy Nelson style and with soft gray eyes that say, "You are the guest I have been waiting for."

"Hey, there. George. George here. Julian," he says, "And how can we help you today?" He waits.

"You," I begin, "have musicians here. So. I know you do. I want to sing. I am really out of practice. You see, I mean, you

134

don't. But, I have this feeling I am to be singing. And I am feeling a bit scared. Really scared. "

He backs up, ushers me inside. "Come in. Sit a spell. What can I get you?"

"Ginger ale. Please." The darkness hides all but our voices. He sits in a long pause.

"I know why you're here."

"You do?"

"Oh, yeah. Easy." He is languid. My ears are up.

"We only get the great ones here," he said that sunlit afternoon, "Street poets and wanderers, homeless men and women, some getting their phd's, loggers who play the blues, and Phillip the puppeteer. And, oh, Eric. You've got to meet Eric." By leaving time, I am part of his family or pantheon of questing folk. No questions asked. He has said, in awe, the name Eric about five times.

"Well, then, hey, I have an idea; a great idea." Hands in the air, dancing a bit. Was he smoking something?

"We have these lunch hours and the atmosphere is easy, laid back. You know? No worries. You come in and play for the folks, you know? Until you get your feet under you. Come in around noon. Okay?"

"Okay. Tomorrow?"

"Tomorrow. Yeah. Now, you must come this Friday night. Eric will be playing. He might even ask you to sing a few songs." .

"Why?" I ask. George was conjuring. I would learn that he was a magnet for bringing together folks from every haunt and place. What was on George's mind? What was on my mind? Fear and excitement and he was daft about Eric.

At the door we stand face to face. Nothing happening. He is now wearing a Willy Nelson smile; he knows somethings. Where I felt pathetic he saw potential. Where I felt out of place he set a table for me. Where I was still playing with the unacceptable failure of a marriage, he knew failure was impossible. His acceptance opened, parachute soft and wide, on the end of his heart.

By the time I left I knew.

I went for the lunches. For the next few weeks I serenade a bevy of white, pink and silver haired ladies who would love me had I spat on the daisies or juggled two oranges, badly. They love everything. They clap when I come and cry when I go. For this faint heart, it is a balm and a sign of what is to come. Women. Mothers all, they know how to praise. They know how to soften the whacks to the heart.

I try out new songs and, day by day, feel the crackling fear fade into a softer knot in my belly. Some call this stage fright. I see it as a relentless abiding distaste for having my shivering entrails seen while buck-naked. As the vocal chords come untied, my quavering voice leaps free. The sadness spins into someone else's world. That's right; I sing out the old sorrows. I sing notes wavering up from an abyss of human confusions that are not entirely my own. It doesn't feel personal. For I feel all the women from all the poems and novels are with me, singing with Ma Rainey, Joni, Judy, Carol, Bessie Smith. All. I bless them. Here it comes, AFLO: (another fecking learning opportunity). The singing brings back a sense of the sweetness of life in gatherings, smiling people, audiences; what I had lost. That wanting to belong. This is new. A landing here from the other side of illness. On the

136

other side of yesterday. Now? I am here. Smack dab in the middle of the unknown.

The following Friday at the Questing Beast I sit in the very back. On stage, his head thrown back, eyes closed, singing loudly, Sugar Magnolia pouring out, is Eric. A long ponytail, large blue eyes and hands which hold this Martin guitar. He has presence or that alchemy called shakti, or a bolting uncharted charisma. He barely contains a voice that comes from an underground well. There is this way he has of phrasing a song that takes him to the edge of the overlook, to the leaning out over that edge, the drop-off always there, and the threat of the fall. The threat of completely losing control.

A cynic and a lover, I will get to know him. We will travel a bit together. He is as wild as the Rogue River and vulnerable as a swallowtail butterfly. What I know now? The voice that cries for love always finds listeners. A voice so full of yearning, carries us together in its rocking and fragile raft. HIs voice carries me past the lyrics and melody into a lowland of desires unmet, of aloneness and a waiting to see and be seen. Then? I was not unlike an animal caged by its own deep melancholy. In him the raw sounds, lurching about, hold out a key, and are carrying a huge backpack of hard knocks and unreachable aching.

"Art is just trying to fill up the huge hole in your center."

Eric's wisdom. Along with Gurdjieff and rock and roll he is among the saved. When he laughs a dam somewhere in Idaho springs a huge leak. Never quite at peace unless sleeping, he was my world, my drama and dharma, for the next eight years. I fell in love with his voice. I fell in step with his pain. I fell in love with Sugar Magnolia. I fell in love. He was living out his passion while moving towards becoming a doctor and Psychiatrist for children. That was his next life. It was a life full of feeling and care.

Then there is Nel, Michael, Ken, Ken Kesey, Marnie, Richard, the Grateful Dead, Anne Bright, Mother Light, Lightning Hopkins, Carol Isis, Marcia, Susan, Terry, Michael Strickland and Michael Graves, all became Oregon for me. All leave their special flavor there. Some are from off and settled in that one horse town in the middle of a valley that was home to the Nez Pierce for many lifetimes. Each brings their wounds, their passions and their unique angles of vision.

Oregon. Her forests tickle my insides and her waters soothe all memories into a day on the Rogue River waiting for the falls. 'Waiting for the falls' needs a melody. There were the trees and the music, the yearning for community, the yearning for something still unknown. Songs of the heart dropped into my whole tribe as we galloped to celebrate, as we galloped out of hiding. We came together to take off the shackles and to wipe the cobwebs and the old ways of seeing from our eyes; from our, at times, mangled questing hearts.

The singers I knew told their truths and let their feelings leak and then explode through their voices. Whole body song I called it; trusting I would find it one day. To love the vibrations that music brought and the loss of a pale reason, and the dancing ignited out of the folk and rock music exploding out of a new generation. I ran through her Forest Park and swam in her waters, ways that kept me sane at a time I was floundering and alone. I thought there was no one there asking or listening. I was wrong.

Eric and I become partners. Nights were music.

The sixties and seventies grew songs like most grow squash; ripe and gleaming with youthful cries, hormones alight and harmonies new and filled with exuberance for living, the land, freedom, Maryjane, magic mushrooms, LSD and community. Eric, his wild laughing and hellbent on rolling through old wounds and old ties. Eric shows me how to free up the voice. Full bodied song like full bodied dancing brings an ecstatic freedom, innocent as Georges' smile. Nights of singing to everyone and no one, something deeper emerged. Something no one named. Some found fame. I found my passions unlocked. Oregon.

The fruits of singing, of music is no different from those of swimming in lakes and riding a horse along a serpentine trail with no end in sight. Or hiking up a mountain till the lungs are bursting into flame. It is to be stripped bare of pretense, it is to be held in the sacred forest, to celebrate letting feelings and breezes rush through, being a part of whatever weathers arise.

Always the question is to the Nameless One to whom we belong. Am I ready for you? Am I worthy? To stand surrounded in wild flowers and sky clad in that wild Oregon was a gift to myself. Here was the feminine, the Goddess, speaking as meadows and forests, as deserts and mountains, as rivers and Native American Indian haunts, and still moving through me if I call her up.

Here I met Erskine Woods, ninety-eight years old and full of spirits of all kinds. As a young boy, he had spent many summers with Chief Joseph of the Nez Pearce. The sons of Chief Joseph had spent time in Oregon with Erskine's father. This is the Chief who saw his family, his tribe, hunted down while on their way to a new home and killed by soldiers out for blood. He finally said, "I will fight no more forever." After that he roamed with his small tribe on a reservation. He had no illusions for he had seen three hundred and sixty treaties with various tribes broken by this America. Now he roams free as an ascended master.

What do I know? Only this, that Chief Joseph and his tribe continue to worship in this valley of pure abundance, continue to listen and gently joggle our elbows if we forget that we are all a part of something mysterious, so magnificent and beyond the minds ken, it has no name. Great Spirit holds it well.

Perhaps they are still instilling us with gratitude for this earth, still singing through us the realization of what it is to be a tribe. To learn from the earth and to take no more than what is needed. For our ways have not led to harmony and listening at earth's heart. I listen to what the elders say. A great nation is one that takes care of its old, its sick and its crippled. A great nation is one that calls the world one family together. For great leaders their word is their honor. A culture of gratitude is its deep song.

Are we learning this song? Shall we harmonize our culture into life and out of suffering again together? Its a choice we have now. Our children need to know the truth of who they are; they know there is an Infinite within them but when they look for truth we give them marketing ideas and money as an antidote to their ills. The native Americans bless the earth while we turn her into a commodity. We put bombs in her womb and call it survival.

Oregon. My first chosen home. Here I sing and have a lover. Here I set up camp as far from my past as possible. Here I sing for three people or for fifty. Did I look back? Yes. Until I could forgive I could not forget. Then? I never looked back. The future had no specific qualities; it was the Bridal Veil Falls, it was a hike through the Cascade Mountains.

For me, then, the future existed as a word. I lived from hour to hour with nothing of my own but the new wardrobe of peasant blouses, hiking boots, Mexican skirts for dancing and jeans; some songs and this expanse of sky in which I felt, finally, and often, at peace.

Breath. Feeling. Sound. Freedom. Fear embraced. Heart openings. Sensuality allowed. An escape from old ways. A foretaste of what a spiritual way offered. Exploring the body directly. Life without a plan. More than that, life without expectations. Geneva kept on winking. I kept on singing. Life without a map.

What is an education without knowing the thousands of messengers of truth, those holy (whole) men and women, whose sole purpose is to enlighten humankind, to take us beyond struggle and to bring us into harmony with our Divine Self? Ancient scriptures speak of Spiritual masters who come down voluntarily from higher realms to serve the world when people are lost. This master is not only the physical embodiment but is also the "divine Self" that pervades the universe. (S)he is Not only the first expression of God but the indwelling "witness" of pure, egoless consciousness that exists beyond the senses and the mind.)

This ever-renewing savior god, whose life, death and sacrifice regenerate the world is part of all the major Mystery traditions. The Egyptian Serapis, the Sumerian Tammuz, the Persian Mithra, the Scandinavian Yimir, the Greek Adonis, the Celtic HU and the Hebrew Lion of Judah. Messengers of truth live lives of complete selflessness. They show us how to live through (h as the presence of love without conditions. Living out of harmony with our natural Self is a struggle.

All messengers re-enact the story of each of us in our quest for mastery. How many know of Sri Babaji? Hilda Charlton? AnandaMai Ma? Lalla? Irina Tweedy? Ammachi? Sister Corita? Peter Ralston? Or the philosopher Paul Brunton? Some are from America. Ammachi is an avatar whose message is of awakening and of self-less service. They come to share liberation from the tangled web of desires, anxieties, fears and ups and downs of living through a persona. The OverSelf is the Divine impulse in a human being; the observer and experiencer of life, which is as the Divine is - immortal.

It is good to have a guide. For what might take two years can takes two minutes with the right guide. -Rumi

After Horse there was a teacher from Calcutta: Dadaji.

I had no interest in meeting him. This was in Oregon around 1973. My friend Nel invited me to a gathering of people, some of whom wanted healing, and others who saw him as a spiritual teacher.

An East Indian man surrounded by ill people? "I'm not sick, Nellie." I told her. That was false. She was a true friend and knew better. I was recovering from an auto accident and was sure that I didn't want to be associated with ill folks or those in recovery. No, I was able to handle things myself. Alone. In the cave. My way.

"Of course, but," she continued in her most soothing, soft voice, "He has siddhis (spiritual powers). You might like him. He was a toy maker in Calcutta until he woke up one day. His guidance was to get out and travel around the world, and tell people who they truly are." I was torn.

Nel told me to meet her at the Twin's house and to bring a large jar of water with a lid. I was working on a documentary film at the time and dealing with a feeling of uselessness, back pain and inertia. The Twins, two sisters with faces sharp and determined as ninjas, had invited many a lecturer and holy man to their house.

"Why the water?" I asked.

"Just bring it," Nel quipped, sounding more mysterious.

"Is he, you know, a Guru?" I asked. Suspicious. Even though the word was new to me, it was a word unused.

"No. He seems to be the opposite. Against all of that."

In truth the word "guru" comes from the root darkness and light. It means the light (of wisdom, of realization) that lights up the darkness. I reflected that Horse had lit up a few candles for me, the night sky another, my grandmother Geneva quite a few more; but here was a teacher who could not speak much English and who asked everyone to bring jars filled with water. So why not? There would be food. And maybe even lassi, my newly discovered Indian rose water drink.

Why not?

I arrived in a kitchen humming with a number of Indian women, their bangles beneath saris, folded into their whispers mixing with the coriander, cinnamon, ginger and cloves as they softly stirred and tasted. On the edge of this spiced world I felt drawn within even as they pointed me to the living room. I had left my bottle of water in the car and told one of them. Her eyes crinkled with delight, as she said, "Ah, yes! It is no problem. I shall tell him later. Just come in, please."

"Where do I Pay?"

"Pay? No money. Your time you are giving, eh? That is the most precious thing you have to give."

With that I was shown into a sun-filled room without furniture. Women from eighteen to eighty were sitting on the floor with bottles – some huge – beside them. Many had shaven heads. Others sat quietly meditating, their bodies withdrawn, their spines sagging in pain, their faces tense with shadows. Nell met me, her large green eyes shining, pulling me down beside her. We sat in the silence of sisters, fingers linked. Then, a noticeable shift; the smell of something, perhaps of flowers wafted through the room. A man followed,

144

covered in vanilla linen, huge dark eyes and a face which seemed fluid and moveable as a mime's. He looked to be around fifty years old. As he stood before us he smiled at each one, in no hurry. Now, the smell of roses is everywhere permeating my skin and clothes. The Twins sit beaming.

He smiles, sits and the questions fly, thanks given, heads bobbed and bowed. Harvey, a pizza shop owner, interprets. At one point the water inside all the bottles sizzles.

"Take off the bottle tops," Harvey says.

From every bottle the roses percolate upward and the room is bathed once again in the fresh scent of roses. Later I learn that he was given this "siddhi" (power) even though he did not ask for it. The smell of roses emanates from his body and aura. He was in truth over seventy years old. What to call it, this presence, this peace that emanated from him? Then, I had need of naming everything, clasping it in words as if that made it clear: Energy. Vibrancy. Peace. Love. Creation. God. Roses. Mystery.

Whatever it was? I knew that I wanted THAT.

I leave early. At the kitchen I stop to ask if I should bring in my bottle. "No," she answers, "but I will tell him."

Driving home, at a stoplight, I hear a sizzling sound in the back seat. I get out to lift the bottle up; It is sizzling with the smell of roses. I take it home and know something truly significant, there are things about which I know nothing whatsoever. I don't know what it is I don't know.

- EB

*

145

Messengers

Realization is not complicated. One need go no place for it, you need not purchase it, you do not have to study it. Realization is so simple, yet profound. It is as if we have been imprisoned all our lives, and all the while the cell door is actually unlocked. The secret is that you have no life without God.

God is within you, living you, giving you *life* twenty-four hours each day. *You can do nothing of your own.* This awareness and acceptance will change your life so drastically that you will have a strength so great as to bear any burden that the unfolding of yourself may bring. *-Dadaji*

 His teaching is simple; the Guru (the light of truth and wisdom) is within. Run from anyone who says they can enlighten you. Know you are not in control. Surrender with every breath. -Dadiji

And? The true Guru is a profound transformer for the one who desires only Reality. Both are true. Truth is paradoxical.

Jesus and the messengers

None of the messengers, the great world teachers who appear to reestablish truth, claimed that they were God. They acknowledged that all souls are expressions of the one light, the one spirit unknowable. The experience of union is our legacy as human/divine beings.

-Dadiji

146

Wonder Questions*

*A wonder question is asked within as you sit. A question
is not given to come up with an answer in words or thoughts; it
may have no answer. Yet always it creates a space in which
something new arises.

Wonder questions from the Way of mastery.

Ask within and you shall be given a hundredfold.

By the depth of your wonder question you shall be
answered. Sometimes these questions collapse the little
mind because it cannot go there. Or, it may be a eureka moment
for you. The ancients and masters from all ways know that these
questions pierce into the depth of your being.

By asking wonder questions I see how the persona mind
works to limit me. 34

Know this, however; if your asking is not in keeping with
the highest good of your purpose here. If it is not in keeping with
the highest good for all creation, I doubt that it shall be fulfilled.
This everywhere Spirit knows your heart and knows what is
needed for you.

Wonder question:

Q: Breathe deeply and ask a wonder question: Am I willing to allow all that is hidden within me to be brought up into the light of consciousness? In this way the mind is purified of what is false and the way becomes one of ease and flow. Am I willing?

Q: Where do I feel incomplete or in lack?

Wonder Questions

Sages all ask questions.

Ramana Maharshi asked me to ask:

Who am I?

Ask yourself this. Do not go into the mind for an answer.

Sit with it.

Wonder question:

Are you aware?

Now, are you aware?

Sit in the power and grace of this question.

Do not go to the intellect for an answer.

The person mind cannot go there.

You join all creation in this knowing:

I exist. I am aware.

What is it about you that does not change?

Dharma

Two thousand years ago, during the Han Dynasty, a man from the west went to China and devoted his whole life to the study and practice of Taoism and a form of Buddhism. His name was Dharma and he resided in the White Horse Temple in the capital of the Han Empire.

His book, *The Text of Altering Nerves* was the result of his life work. Dharma stated that to remain youthful, we must exercise our nerves to reverse deterioration and to preserve softness and expandability. Yoga asanas (ways of being) also help the nerves to remain vital.

Dharma believed that all human problems came from problems related to the nervous system. Dharma gave us exercises that soften, strengthen and expand our nervous system. The nerves are an intricate network of "communication cables" connecting our brain to our organs. When nerve impulses slow, mental and physical process are slow. This is aging.

He is a servant of humanity, of the Common good.

memoir - Zen Basketball - David Zucker

1974 - Cape Cod.

The most remarkable day of Basketball I ever spent.

I am 25 years old, riding my new 10-speed bike on a 70 mile trip from Boston to Cape Cod, for the weekend. Going with Pierre and David, two other members of the Boston Repertory Theatre. 3:00am, we set off south along the back roads leading to the cape. Still dark and the cool emptiness of the city is oddly comforting.

We make our way smoothly and easily down streets that usually feel more like an obstacle course with double-parked trucks, taxis, commuters, diesel fumes and pedestrians. The buildings gradually give way to suburban houses and trees and hills! Cape Cod sure has a lot of steep hills for a sandbar.

We stop along the way for muffins and coffee, enjoying each other's company and the unique-to-bicycles experience of whisper quiet traveling through nature. Eventually we make our way over the Sagamore Bridge onto the cape and then to Barnstable and Louie's house, Pierre's brother.

In the afternoon, David, Pierre, and I decide to play several games of GHOST in the driveway of (Pierre's brother) Louie's, house.

For those of you who don't know the game... Each person takes a turn shooting the ball at the basket. If you sink your shot, the person after you has to shoot the exact same shot. If they miss, they get a "G". Each time a player misses a shot made by the person before them, they get a letter of the word, "Ghost." All five letters and they are out of the game. If, however, you miss your shot, the next person gets a free shot; they don't have to do yours.

I turn in my usual average-mediocre-disappointing-to-me performance. I am better at making unpressured "free" shots than I am at duplicating my opponent's successes. When the pressure's on to sink a shot that the person before me has made I choke and miss. Each game we play I am the first one out.

After several games under an increasingly hot sun, Pierre and David decide to go to the beach to cool off. I am frustrated and angry at myself. I decide to stay there and shoot baskets.

I have just finished reading Eugen Herrigal's <u>Zen in the Art of Archery</u>. It has become my bible as to how to approach life and art. In the book it says that the arrow releases itself. Success or failure in the art of archery has to do more with the release of the arrow than with whether or not the arrow hits the target.

Focusing on the *process* of releasing the arrow, rather than the *goal* of hitting the bulls-eye, actually results in more bulls-eyes. The master archer knows he has hit the bulls-eye even before the arrow is released! I understand the concept, but how to make it happen?

I become determined to apply the principles of Zen Archery to my basketball game. The ball is my arrow, the hoop my bulls-eye. I am going to focus on the process of releasing the ball, not on whether or not the ball goes through the hoop. The process *is* the goal.

It's not so easy to redirect years of focusing on the goal to focusing on the process. But I am frustrated and angry enough with myself to make me determined to carry on. (too angry and frustrated and I would have gone to the beach).

For the next three hours straight I shoot baskets, dissolving any sense of expectation of the ball going in; dissolving any illusory sense of a relationship existing between one shot and the next, so that even if I make six or seven baskets in a row, it doesn't mean that I can't make the next one. Each shot, each moment in time exists all by itself not depending on the shot/moment before it or influencing the shot/moment coming after.

What is most important is releasing the ball and *feeling my way towards the basket.* "Before the arrow is released, the bulls-eye is already hit." As I practice shooting, this concept becomes reality, Truth.

I begin to embody it.

I make a body-mind-feeling-ball-hoop connection. I and the basket are one! I know the ball is going into the basket before I even release it. I have rubber arms that stretch over space and literally stuff the ball into the basket from a distance... It is that clear and that definite a knowing. Wow! I am the embodiment of the book. I DID IT!

At the same time a part of me is aware of how tenuous this connection is. Any fear of failure, the slightest desire to make the shot causes mental and physical tension, results in a feeling of separation between myself and the basket, and I miss.

As long as I sustain the body-mind-emotions-ball-basket connection there is no room for thoughts of gain or loss to creep in. The *feeling* is all. The feeling is my awareness of everything around me *as* Me, it is the 'State of Grace' from the Catholic catechisms of my youth. It is what drives all spiritual seekers, saints, mystics, poets, artists, warriors,... Nothing can equal this feeling of union.

Most of the time the ball doesn't even touch the rim. I am like a laser-guided missile; wherever the ruby light of my intention is aimed, the ball follows... automatically. I just keep feeling-shooting -scoring.

Eventually David and Pierre come back from the beach. They are startled to see me still playing. I ask if they want to play another game. They agree, teasing me about how good I should be now with so much practice. I am excited to see if I can sustain my State of Grace under the additional threat of competition.

We play three games. I don't miss one have-to-make shot. I never even get the first 'G' of GHOST.

I am visited by Mastery on this day.

It is forever holy to me.

Attuning with your True Self.

How various traditions voice attunement with the Infinite.

Bhagavad-Gita: *Krishna to Arjuna: Continuously absorb your heart in me.*

Mystic Christ: *Pray without ceasing. Be still and know that*
I AM God. Be present and in deep feeling-communion within.

Advaita-non dual: *It is not difficult. Leave the mind outside. Leave the past and future on the shelf. Come into being awareness which is pure knowing.*

Native American: *Great Spirit is all and everywhere. And ever-unfolding. All is sacred. All is holy. There is only Great Spirit.*

All: *Relax into this Presence. Become Present with what is arising. Now. As it is. Deepen into the stillness within. Have no expectations, yet, be expectant. There is only the One Spirit of Life. Know your Self and you know God.*

EB: *Say yes and sing or say Alleluia a few times for no reason whatsoever.*

Wonder question:

If you knew that there are no mistakes and nothing is random, that everything is brought to you by your own spirit, would you see challenging events and people from your life in a new light?

Write about it in your journal. Talk to a friend. Bring out into the light the miracles of this life that are not in your control. Begin to purify the mind of the habit of taking things for granted, believing in circumstance rather than in your indwelling spirit who is always drawing you closer to home - your True Nature.

The wonder inquiry is:

    Where do I feel lack in my life?

    The feeling of lack is a prime program among human

        beings.

    There lies my edge.

    And, I awaken at my edge.

    The universe as created is abundant.

    There is no lack of love, guidance, wealth, or food.

    If I feel lack I am in the world of the persona/ego. And the

        ego arises from fear.

    In God's world there is only abundance.

Wonder questions:

Is there a truth I am not sharing with someone?
Is there a truth I am not sharing with myself?
Secrets mean I feel special; or I feel unworthy.
Either way, bring up all your secrets,
share together, laugh together.

Where do I resist the truth of who I am?
Where in the body does the breath not go?
As you breathe look to the inner sensations:

Where is there tightness; in the throat, the belly, the back?
The body shows you where you are armored, where there
is resistance to the flow of the breath, the flow of life.

Where there is resistance to the breath, the flow of feeling
and aliveness is diminished. There is an old program coming up for
acceptance, for healing.

Wonder question:

Take a few minutes after your breathing. Sit and ask
yourself these wonder questions:

How do I spend most of my time?
Do I spend time worrying about money or a mate or the
future or the body?

What do I truly value?
This is the same question as how do I spend most of my
time?

What are the beliefs that run my life?
Knowing that the body is the mirror of the mind. Knowing
that your body reflects the thoughts, beliefs and programs you are
living by.

memoir - In Pursuit of the Tiger

There are no accidents. Only meetings. -eb

Portland, Oregon 1973.

A spring day in the early seventies. I am driving down off the west hills outside of Portland, Oregon, singing. The breeze is soft on my face, I am harmonizing with James Taylor, "I've seen fire and I've seen rain. But I always thought I'd see you again." I know now how good life is. A singer, I spend my nights wailing out sorrows and joys to the songs of Buffalo Springfield, the Grateful Dead, Joanie Mitchell, Bonnie Raitt.

A truck appears too soon on my windshield. We twirl together to the squeals of sparks and bent steel. Nick, a teen-age boy, had driven through a stop sign. With that my life changes directions. Where I had spent my days moving, running, riding, hiking, dancing and singing, now? I can hardly walk for the pain. My spine spasms for months. They put me in a cast and afraid to touch me. My body vomits up pain killers and muscle relaxers. Drugs and my body do not dance well.

I am, in that blink of collision, a bonafide mess. So I begin to sit. I begin to read. I begin to feel into myself in ways only pain, solitude and sitting can bring. I am inconsolable. I will try anything but more doctors.

A friend, in touch with the new, takes me to a class, something called, "Yoga." There I find Giselle teaching the strangest of routines. She asks me to accept it all. All that has happened and all that I am. Resist nothing.

"But how can I love this broken back?" I ask.

Pregnant she falls over doing the tree asana, laughs hugely and resets herself. "Breathe in the pain, allow it to be." She touches me in the way that another will touch me, at the heart chakra. The tears continue to pour out. All that I had stuffed away; the years of feeling alone, of feeling a foreigner in my family, of looking for, no, yearning, for the truth behind the facades of the world. Truth. Reality. God? I could not say. My vision quest was in hiding. As were so many old fears and programs.

Growing up I spent hours riding through meadows and asking questions. Was it a real family I yearned for? No. There was still the feeling of being guilty, of having done something shameful. What? The isolation I put on myself and the real loneliness which comes of being shut down were not conscious realities. Now? This flow of energy begins to pour through me.

With the discipline of the breath and slow asanas, energies begin to move through my spine and back again. The pain lessens. As I breathe the Yoga breaths, called Pranayam, everyday, the pain begins to fade. I need no pills. This is my first amazing discovery. Healing comes. Once again, I walk and run, ride and dance. Giselle. Her gentle and loving kindness becomes a beacon. Some of her sayings become my mantras. For awhile. She quits teaching to have her baby. A new life with a new vision quest..

As I wander in the Yoga realms there are teachers who know some technique, some who know how to be pretzels, others who know how to strip the spirit out of Yoga to comply with fitness routines. There are those who teach it as a rote enterprise and those who know how to dive into the stillness and the inward gaze. All perfect. You will meet them.

Later, as I wander through this world of Yogas - Iyengar, Kripalu, Bikram, Power, Ashtanga, Vinyasa, her light continues to shine, pure and unassailed. Like Horse, she taught me about breath. Seeing life through the heart, rather than the head, was the only way. My time with Yoga was used to open, to hold an asana, breathe the ujjayi breath and know a very real emergence of energy, of vitality and at times? Of bliss and ecstasy.

The family was not interested.

Bliss and ecstasy were the foretaste, the carrot on the stick the universe used. Yes. I was all for allowing new experiences. All for opening up. "Give it to me Lord! I am ready." No-holds- back was now my middle name. Or Bliss girl.

I came to see that Yoga is about loving with no conditions, me and all creation. Voila, Giselle. Voila, Jesus. Voila Ramana Maharishi. Babaji. Anandamai Ma. Voila. An easy message. On ears only half open. It was beyond me; I was waiting for something to happen. The fire of truth was rolling and I was being burned. My parents were sure I was in a cult. In Texas a Yoga teacher was run out of town and labelled 'Satan." Ignorance is everywhere. Approval is nowhere.

Meantime...

That year, after the accident, is a meantime year. I bided my time, waiting for inspiration for the future. I needed to breathe. That was it. Breathing made space between my words. Space between my thoughts. Space between the hurting ribs. Space between me and my family. Space between me and a feeling of dread never quite voiced. The old program arose that I was not going to be on this earth for long. Breathe deeply and be free. And so I breathed and the body healed.

Wonder questions:

> What conditions must there be in my life for
> me to be at peace?
> On whom do I project my power?
> From whom do I seek approval?

Wonder Q:

> *What part of myself am I unable to accept?* (dis-associate

from)

At the end of a loves breath or while you are waiting for your tea at Starbucks, ask a question within. The answer will come. You may feel a sense of presence, perhaps not in words; perhaps you will meet an old or new friend, a teacher, a film may bring the answer.

Holy Spirit uses all of the world's symbols (forms) to bring you what you need. In each moment begin to cultivate asking within. Cultivate the intuition, the still small voice of spirit.

I always look to be surprised.
Be surprised.

Wonder questions:

What is the primary element of all experience?
  What cannot be taken from you,
    even as you leave the body?

Sit with this. It is the one thing that permeates everything,
  it is that which comes before all else.

Of myself I can do nothing. Yet, through me Father/Mother
  God does all things.

What is this Father/Mother God? Truly?
It is this mystery of beingness.
Let go of trying to capture it through the persona mind.
As Neem Karoli Baba says, "Just see God in everything -
  don't try to figure it out."

It is that which moves through you,
It is the doer and the maker.

There is nowhere that the Infinite Source, the Divine, is not.

165

memoir - Breathing light

I'm Nobody! Who are you?
Are you—Nobody—Too?
Then there's a pair of us!
Don't tell! they'd banish us—you know!
How dreary—to be—Somebody!
How public—like a Frog—
To tell one's name—the livelong June—
To an admiring Bog!   -Emily Dickinson

Currents of energy keep moving through me. The sense of struggle is no longer center stage. Seeking was continual and being alert to what flowed into my life. I began asking for a Yoga teacher.

Tom Stiles, a remarkable Yoga teacher in Boston, taught Vinyasa Yoga after the lineage of Desikacharya, the son of the great Krishnamacharya, giver of most all Yogas in our time. The truth behind the three rivers of Yoga, Vinyasa, Ashtanga and Iyengar, is that Krishmacharya gave each man the perfect Yoga for his own constitution and personality. Very different men and very different approaches to Yoga.

My companion, Michael Graves, had asked me to move east to be together. In what way? I enrolled in Tom Stiles Vinyasa Yoga Teachers Training, which included anatomy, asana, some yoga therapy, and pranayama (breathing). I continued sitting an hour each morning and an hour each night. I went to the mat as I went to ride my horse, expectant and my heart opened wide. This discipline that takes years to inhabit felt already a part of me. So I moved back east to Boston with a feeling of having found; I would become a Yoga teacher.

It felt sane and right. I did not know yet what it was to have a tiger by the tail. I would learn. Yes, we all learn.

The years of being a student again, of receiving a certification were full and rich. Unlike college where I studied the world and its thinkings and doings, how to navigate it, sing and do art and still allow abundance, ah, the rub. Here, I was learning about Being. The paradox of it kept me alert, kept me aware.

Still, this niggling belief of being unprepared; how could I really call myself a Yoga teacher? It felt presumptuous. It sounded professional and pretentious. Those Indian Hindu yogis with the soft brown eyes and flowing hair spent their days in postures and meditation; teaching was an offshoot of their love of God, their way of being in the world.

Yes, I liked how I felt; the aliveness, the powerful currents of energy and then the calmness coming out of the Warrior, Cobra or bridge asanas. But God? God was still something else for me; something fearful. Without God, yoga was merely about postures. And hadn't I tried enough of those in my life? Posturing to be someone? Still, I would have to be perfect for the divine to accept me into the kingdom. There was something I was running from. What was it?

In truth? I was afraid, yes, afraid of my very own self. Afraid even of what would emerge from sitting in silence. The Hero's journey includes dropping down into the deepest cave, into the underground. What will emerge? What old fear or demon?

I learned soon that the fear I have of this inner Self, that fear I project onto the Creator. Yes, it gets complicated when I try to figure it out with the little mind! This was the rub. I feared what was hanging out in my sub-conscious. While the

Infinite One? THAT was something too wondrous for this questioning being.

Yet, deep within I knew that the ascended ones talk and whisper to us. We are simply vessels for the one voice within all of creation. Why is there all this confusion and struggle? Is it because we run away from who we truly are? We cannot be with "what is;" we cannot be the Presence of the Infinite because we feel too small? Or is it that God is way far away having left his wretched creation alone and fairly confused. And so we look for dramas instead. Mind keeps me fascinated with the material world, the diverse forms, its dramas, its films, its things and people that come and go. Living from the persona is dysfunctional and only leads to suffering.

At times I was called to allow shame and sadness to move through me. Along with this is the realization that I am one with and surrounded by a creation alive with the light of my own soul. This Light that you are, that I AM, is ONE. Yet, who could truly know our magnificence, then?

Know that God's essence is all of creation.

"Once you love God, you love this creation; and then you do not hate anymore." [35]

FALL

Trust and surrender

When you finally let go you will find there is a net, that was always there, invisible and loving. It will bring you into pure knowing and it will bring you home. You cannot 'figure it all out'; impossible. Yet, you can trust. The leap is into complete trust. The leap is in complete surrender to THAT which birthed you out of it's Self, THAT which holds you and is **You** at your core.

For when you are living in the space of the Beholder, the one who blesses, the one who is in Presence with all that arises, there is nothing to fear. There is nothing that can threaten the holy Self of you.

It is exhausting to stay in control all of the time.
It is exhausting not to trust.
It is exhausting to worry over the lives of everyone as if you are responsible for the world and its problems.

I began to simply give friends, family, students and events over to Spirit. Some call it prayer. Sometimes I merely ask Amma, the Divine Mother. Or Abba, Mother/Father God - the OverSoul.

Gatherings are like that. Breaths are like that.

At a certain point all teachers simply let go of the teaching. Forget about why they are there. Before each Yoga class, as I check in with my own inner sensations, my body responds and the sense of being or spirit, what comes through is not of the mind's memory but of that deeper place within.

Oftentimes I have no memory of what takes place in a class, just a soft feeling of flow within myself and through the entire room. And, I trust, through all gathered there.

Real gatherings are like that; everyone is there for the purpose of allowing and surrender; as we relax into the moment, what follows is a letting go of resistance. What follows is often a mystery.

For me? A realization that existence is a mystery, even as I come into Presence and feel the flow of spirit pull me deeper within. What I know? I am in the right place. Exactly the right place.

Yoga is knowing the stillness. It is not simply within you.

You are the stillness.

I no longer looked for quiet places. After years of being in Presence and diving deeper, the quiet takes over. Here is the funniest thing of all; the breathing stops. A deep and subtle movement within but no lung breathing. Perfect.

The three best known Yoga styles taught in the West today can be traced back to one master teacher, Tirumalai Krishnamacharya.

"Inhale, and God approaches you. Hold the inhalation, and God remains with you. Exhale, and you approach God. Hold the exhalation, and surrender to God."   -

Krishnamacharya

"Master your breath, let the self be in bliss, contemplate on the sublime within you."   *-Krishnamacharya*

Messengers of truth and breath

Messengers of truth and breath

"If one's inhalations and exhalations are not balanced, one loses the harmonious breath energy of heaven and earth. This is how diseases are produced.   -Taoist Text

Two well-known teachers who include breathing as part of their wisdom teachings are the Buddha and Jeshua Ben Joseph/ Jesus.

The Buddha

Shakyamuni Buddha wanted only one thing; to realize his True Self. He tried many approaches before he came to the breath.

It is said that Buddha practiced meditation and extreme asceticism between age twenty-nine (when he decided to take on the spiritual path), and age thirty-five (when he reached enlightenment). Training methods back then were accompanied by pain, effort and straining. Buddha disciplined himself by meditating under the burning sun, being naked in cold weather, fasting, holding his breath, and so on. He totally devoted himself to this training for six years.

Finally, he was led to a new realization: "The harsh training only made me weak and thin to a point that I was bones and skin. I reached no enlightenment, and it was a very wasteful action." What does the "holding breath" technique do to you? Everyone knows that if you forcefully stop the breath for too long you suffocate and die.

After repeating such experiences Buddha quit the training. As stated in the sutra, which is depicted in the ancient Buddhist text of *Samyutta Nikaya,* the Buddha began to sit and follow the breath.

The Aramaic Jesus
Jeshua ben joseph (Jesus)

Jeshua Ben Joseph spoke Aramaic. He lived in a village in the Middle East where people lived by certain traditional and unquestionable codes: the main one being the unity of all things. The individual is part of a family, which is part of a community, which is part of a village, a country and a cosmos. All is one with the Lord (shimmering presence of loving oneness- translation from the Aramaic.)

He travelled extensively; documented records trace him to Egypt, India, and Tibet with the Buddhists. The hidden Jesus is only now coming into the light of day. He spent years before his ministry began with esoteric masters from various traditions and countries.

His coming was foretold by at least five masters from different spiritual traditions including Buddha and Zoroaster. He was seen as part of a larger plan to heal world consciousness - both then and now. The Vatican has some of these records. "Issa" was the name given Jeshua in Tibet. He lived unconditional love and taught how to "attune" to the Divine within. Many see him at the center of a Divine plan whose threads run through all esoteric and spiritual paths.

"Yet few teacher's words of peace, oneness, self-knowing and realizing the Kingdom of God within have ever been so misinterpreted to create conflict, wars and persecution."[36]

In the four canonical gospels Jesus refers to "Spirit" more than one hundred times.

God is breath.
All that breathes resides in the Only Being.
From my breath
To the air we share
To the wind that blows around the earth
Sacred Unity (God as One) inspires all.[37]

In both Hebrew and Aramaic, the same word – 'ruha' in Aramaic and 'ruach' in Hebrew – stands for many English words: Spirit, wind, air, and breath. When we meditate on the words of a mystic or prophet in the Middle Eastern way, we must consider all possibilities simultaneously. For as in the tradition of the midrash, there are layers of meaning – one word does not suffice. So "Holy Spirit" must also be "Holy Breath."

Aramaic translations of Jeshua's words in Greek and Latin do not include the ground of meaning inherent in the Middle East culture of that time.

"Sacred unity" is how He, Jeshua Ben Joseph, puts it. In the Middle East there is only the realization of unity. Even the idea of mind, body and spirit has no place in their knowing.

The separation between body and spirit, between the Creator and the created that we find in the western Latin and Greek languages is not a part of the tradition from which Jesus was birthed. Nowhere is it more evident than contrasting the Lord's Prayer translated from the latin, and the same prayer called, "Prayer to the Lord" translated from the Aramaic.

PRAYER TO THE LORD Aramaic

Jeshua gave this prayer in answer to the question from his friends: How do we attune to the Divine? It was a teaching tool. It is a celebration of our oneness with the one shimmering Light.

Ah-bwoond'bwash-maya Neeta-kadsha schmach
Tay-tay malkoota.
Ne-whay t'save-ya-nach eye-janna d'brash op-baraha
How-lahn lachma d-soonkahnan yow-manna
Wash wo-klan how-bane eye-kanna dap haknan shaw-ken
el'high-ya-bane. Oo-lah tahlan el'mees-yo-na,
  ella pahsahn min beesha
Metahl dilahkee malkoota ll-high-la, ooteech-bohkta-ta
La-alahm all-meen, al-men, amen

PRAYER TO THE LORD English translation from the Aramaic

Father-Mother of the Cosmos, Shimmering Light of All.

Your light forever within us as we breathe your Holy Breath.

In the sanctuary of our hearts, You are uniting within us the sacred rays of your Power and Beauty.

Let your heart's desire unite heaven and earth through our sacred union.

Help us fulfill what lies within the circle of our lives today.

Forgive our secret fears as we freely choose to forgive the secret fears of others.

Let us not enter forgetfulness, tempted by false appearances.

For from your Astonishing Fire comes the Eternal Song which sanctifies all, renewed eternally in our lives, and throughout Creation.

We seal these words in our hearts, committed in trust and faith.

Amen, ameyn, almen.

The prayer in Aramaic posits that: Your Light, Lord*, penetrates our being right NOW. Love is the energy, the Spirit of all Creation. Your Holy Breath makes us whole. It is the Life Essence, which is everywhere at once.

*In Aramaic the term 'Lord" means "shimmering Presence of Loving Oneness." It is unfolding through you and through all creation at this moment. the queendom (malkoota – fertile field of creating). As we breathe, as we feel into the heart and out of the ego-mind, we make ready for Holy Spirit to guide through us. This Prayer tells us all about this simple yet often hidden teaching of Jesus.

God is not off in a far heaven. The Shimmering Presence is here and now. I am not a sin-filled creature. Sin, guilt and fear were never a part of his life; he was here to bring the joy, excitement, aliveness of what it is to be in attunement with the Infinite. No need for salvation for we are the offspring of the One. We are an expression of all that is, this field of the divine, of the Lord.

Jeshua Ben Joseph shares two things through this Prayer of the Lord:
1) Reveals the nature of all things. Revealing that our breath is the bridge to attuning with this Cosmic loving energy which is everywhere at one.
2) Shares that the infinite Source of Life is constantly pouring Itself into Its creation, and this alone allows all created things to exist.

I chose to include the Prayer for two reasons:
-The misunderstanding of what Jeshua Ben Joseph taught has led to so many battles and conflicts throughout our world. In most spiritual literature, battles are metaphors for the one true battle; that which takes place in the heart of humans between the ego voice and the voice for love. As an Ascended Master he continues to speak through many.
-The Lord's Prayer in Aramaic includes much of his teaching. "Love they neighbor as thyself" and "love one another as I have loved you." These are truly the very heart of his message when he was embodied. Love is without conditions. It is the substance of beingness, life itself. Often he says, "You are the Presence of Love in form." How can it be other? How did we miss this for so long?

Jeshua Ben Joseph/Jesus teaches that all human/divine beings are Christ or Christed spirit.

'Christ' is an ancient word, part of the Mystic tradition, and means that soul who knows no separation only oneness. It is the Universal Christ in which all are. That Soul who is not fragmented but whole or holy awakens as the Christ.

"Sin" is being off the path of Self realization, off the path of knowing your Self. It is a call to come into love without conditions. It is also called Christ consciousness, Cosmic consciousness, Buddha mind, God consciousness.[38]

Jeshua Ben Joseph was a Jewish Rabbi.
He is not a Christian.
Buddha is not a Buddhist.
Reflect.
Jeshua Ben Joseph continues to teach and talk
        with those who ask.

Have you asked?

Creation is not a clock wound up at the beginning.
It is occurring, fresh, new and eternal in every moment.
It is intimate, alive, innocent, wondrous, beautiful,
And over-flowing with the grace-filled revelation
That GOD IS.
Outpouring of Love is the inherent shape of the universe.

Christ (is the masterpiece of love in the midst
of a creation designed for love, not a divine plumber come
to fix the mess of original sin.

The Infinite has never stopped speaking through various
prophets of all cultures.
Ask within a question and you shall be given the answer.
Trust.

Health, Healing and Presence

Children
We are here to celebrate all creation and all beings. ¬way of mastery

A child comes in complete and with a purpose. All your lives have helped to shape this life; so be aware and alert to all that comes onto your path. The child is not a blank slate but has his own indwelling spirit, her own purpose and unique vision quest. The child is in a state of love and looks to the family to support his passion, her life, their path. By seeing the child's perfection, by giving it your love without conditions, the child sees her own perfection in your reflecting light. You are his God and mentor on how to be in the world and what to value.

Hitting or yelling at a child closes down the nervous system. Nurturing and uplifting will cause the child to go forth with self-acceptance, excitement and a desire to excel. Never push or shove them in your direction - they have their own deep seated being, exuberant to show itself, exuberant to live this life completely and to fulfill their purpose. Their way. Which is none of your business.

No system of education can be complete if one omits teaching children how to be in Presence. This one art will assist them to develop self-control, improve character and to master all the other arts through mastery of concentration. Knowing that the Great Spirit of life lives within them and expresses itself as all creation, gives them a compass when life gets turbulent.

As a child I often lived with my grandparents, Geneva and Big Daddy. These memories come backlit by the wild sea grasses and the waves lapping and keeping time with the child's beating heart. That child knew eternity, then, and it came with the seabirds and the sure footprints in the sand of this large, unpredictable and comfortable woman called Nevie. Of all their homes there was this cottage on Sullivan's Island. Held by crashing waves, murmured to by the wind and blessed by scores of seabirds who circle in to catch the bread bits she throws up for them. Safety. I never felt so much a part of a place, a family and a simplicity as then. Dressed In her cotton polka dot dress that flares up around her face of milk and sky she presides still over the sea and every room that holds a piano. She is the Priestess of compassion, morality and arrowroot cookies which fall from a bottomless pocket of her dress.

As we walk to the shore, Geneva turns over the sand dollar that I hand her. Every object is a place of myth and curiosity.

"So look at this, Ms. Bits, these four petals are like the directions, north, south, east and west. Like a flowery cross. Planted in the earth yet open to the winds and weather and to heaven. Now, let me tell you something; no one is going to help you. These petals give you the directions. But no one tells you which way to go. You are here all by yourself. Especially you. Do you see? So there you are." She sees something even then that I would only know later. The aloneness woven into my fantasies and longings, my love of the piano, singing and reading, the disorganization, the wanting of love in a family without compass and the muses of wandering who hurried me along. Years later, as she lay in the hospital, the liver cancer doing a cracking good job, she comes out of a deep sleep with a broad smile and her sky-blue eyes blinking wide to find me.

"Do I look sick to you?" She threw the words out. I went numb. "But its just not so, my child. Now you listen to me: don't you believe everything you see or hear. They lie. This body is just a snakeskin; its got to be shucked off. Inside I am as strong as a herd of wild horses." .

"A herd of wild horses?" I asked, in shock.

"Now don't you mimic what I say." She winks again. All my tears stop. Even the pain and sadness crumple into dust.

Don't believe everything you see. There's a realm behind it all that gives it the luster and the gas, and don't think you can take it away by pretending something else. Loose translation of last words. I wondered.

Did she say that just for me and my fears? Would she forego a chance to teach? No. I knew her well. Feelings were less important to her than truth. It was her own brand but never, ever, throughout our twenty-seven years together did she ever qualify anything to make someone feel good. If anything she upped the ante to get her point across. Music, truth, art and love of my grandfather, these dominated her life and conversation.

*

Then there was Thomas. Always present, he sits in a locked trunk in a basement room of our family tree, well out of sight. He sits as a call to everyone to listen and to reflect. Spirit, as it comes into the physical, takes on flesh and takes on many forms. He came into this world also a human/divine being but deranged in mind and with a crooked body; he was a giant without boundary. She kept him at home, sat him at the piano with me to learn our scales together. She served us our milk toast and tried to keep him from sitting on me. A useless enterprise.

Beyond this mundane world, she waited. In her mother's

heart was one vibrating string, glory bound, which was not tied off; on it was the belief and prayer that one day those fingers would burst free and play a Mozart sonata. Play it from the heart. Perfectly. The Idiot Savant secreted in the discordant body. Tireless, unstoppable, she pitched forth between us as we perched on the stool and played, Tom on her left and me on her right. We grapple and bang and slobber and call out, "Muvah! Muhva!" until he is locked away to continue banging and screaming and then a fall into a sleep.

Piano came easily to me as I sat on the high pitched keys and Thomas on the low ones. As I hear piano music today I also see her, high Priestess of music and I see him, never banished and never out of hearing. He was my Uncle and he was her son. He stands at every doorstep as both the beast and the divine, both her fate and her treasure. She loved him as he was. She knows his perfection, just as she loves me. The image explodes, how love embraces all, accepts all. All. I looked to the world for a map of meaning. She sent me there; when I finally turned to see her, she winks. Her hand on her heart, beyond time and space.   -EB

O human, see the the human being rightly: the human being has heaven and earth and the whole of creation in itself, and yet is a complete form, and in it everything is already present, though hidden.   -Hildegard von Bingen

The Luminous Being

Pondering

The body is simply a field of condensed consciousness.

The human energy field or Biofield is composed of layers
of consciousness, interwoven and pulsating both through and
surrounding what seems like a material body.

You are a field of consciousness which has no limits.
Healing takes place here.

The body is simply a modulation of this field. All forms are
modulations of this field of awareness. The majority of the field is
continually being bathed by the ever ongoing flow of the Infinite
Source. Some call this the Biofield. Some call it consciousness,
the Oversoul or Self.

As it descends from spirit through our energy fields into the
lower frequency of the body, it carries messages and information.
The natural flow of Source/Essence is through the heart chakra.
Yet, collectively, most of humanity depends upon the persona/ego
mind; we go here first for guidance. We forget our heart
connection.

Healing

Western medicine sees life as beginning and ending with biology and the physical body. Yet, physicists tell us, there is no such thing as matter; there is only energy vibrating at different frequencies.

Traditional cultures look beyond the chemical interactions to the underlying energy/cosmic life force that vitalizes all of life. This life force pervades the cosmos and manifests in every individual organism: plants insects, animals, human beings and all of creation. It is the power which creates suns and planets and keeps entire solar systems moving in symmetry and harmony.

The Chinese know this life force as *chi* (also qi), the Hindus call it *prana*; the Greeks call it *pneuma*. The mystic Christ calls it h*oly Spirit*. It is called light, energy, consciousness or pure awareness.

All ancient healing systems are founded on the principles that in order to heal the body, the person must harmonize the flow of life energy within.

Breath first, feeling and heart next, mind last
Deep breathing connects you to the life around you.

In Presence

As you sit, leave off thoughts of who you think you are. You are not your name. You are not your story. Let them go. Be here with what is arising. Attend to the field of sounds as they come and go. The feeling sensations of the body, come and go. If the breath is the body of God, then this field of beingness is also this body. No separation.

Let your attention come to the feeling of being, of existing. This aware ever-present field. Feel it as a cloud of shimmering life, or beingness emanating through and around, a spaciousness.

Pondering

All that appears as form are various modulations of the universal consciousness - the universal Essence. The ground of all existence. Beingness itself. The body appears to be a bit more dense and this delusion continues to create a scenario of seeming separation between objects. As we experience the truth, through relaxing into Presence, Reality reveals itself. You must experience this for yourself.

Experience the body as an offshoot of the mind. The mind is an offshoot of consciousness. The body is a modulation of consciousness. The body is a bit more dense as all forms are various frequencies of the same stuff -

Health of the body is really health of the mind. As for the body is an offshoot of our thoughts and beliefs about ourself, the world, others and creation. The body is an offshoot of mind. Mind is an offshoot of consciousness. Consciousness itself is the unified field, the ground of all being and existence. All experiencing is going on solely within consciousness.

memoir - Grace

Harvard, Massachusetts, 1990
Bare Hill Pond

At 4:00 AM on a bright fall day in 1990 I sit. Not unlike other mornings I do some asanas, breathe my Kriya breath and then, I sit.

The pond shimmers back at me as the Canada geese parade their new goslings along the shore. No peace follows. A restlessness curdles the body and mind. What arises this morning? Frustration. There is fear of the future and anger and then despair; and they are all percolating through me in equal degrees. For me, they are demons without pity. I watch them arise to slam my chest, tighten my throat and move throughout my belly. Tears come. I want to run and hide somewhere. Hey, listen, hear me, how do I get off this planet? That old theme of escape. Welcome, my old friend.

Resistance is impossible. Resistance is futile.

Unlike other mornings I choose to put aside all that I thought I knew. That includes Yoga, meditation, my life, the peace and the questions. I choose to know nothing and expect nothing.

I voiced it all. "Look here, listen up, what is going on? Why am I this cauldron, this sad, selfish plate of emotions. Look, I have done it all pretty good. Okay. And still this? This anger, this feeling of being wrong, unloveable and then more frustration." Bubbling over, the fury unspent, I breathe as the feelings move through me. Yes, I am angry. I am angry with God.

Here was the program; I had been brought into life against my will and left alone and unsupported. I had looked for a noble purpose in life, read all the right books, become a Yoga teacher; I was in love, I was singing and writing songs and yet? It wasn't enough?

Am I an ingrate? These emotions, these feelings of having failed that erupt out of, well, where? A mystery. I wanted to know what it was all about. As I looked at those pictures of Indian gurus I sometimes felt "less than". Here they are, chocolate colored and pure peace enwrapped in vanilla robes, devout with that inward gaze, the world gone, holy others inviting us to join with them. Sure thing.

What I didn't feel was that God was "listening" to me, as She was to everyone else. Left out, on the fringe, moving through life oarless. Yes, this is a familiar feeling from childhood, returning again; left to roam around on my own, unseen and unsupported.

Some mornings, the bed seemed my only friend. At times so drenched by emotions I feel my insides are a battlefield in a blinding hailstorm; at times a sadness so deep the stars took on my misery. Everyday a tumult, a truce and a chaos. And another truce. The grand schism I call it. Loving God brings up all the falseness, all the pretense of the persona.

Getting tough with the Nameless One was not my way. Yet, Yogananda, whose teachings had brought me to breathe and to sit, had said that, as the holy child of the Creator, you might want to, well, demand.

Demand? Okay, I demand. So here am I, and I demand. I felt arrogant. Then I felt empowered. I smiled. I laughed.

A veil lifted

Yogananda writes in his Christmas message that Jesus comes to him at this time of the year. The consciousness of humankind is more open and loving than at other times. He and Jesus speak. You must know here that Krishna and a long list of Yogi/Christs also come to him. He is as pure and transparent as an Alaskan waterfall; and so they come.

"Ask Jesus to come to you," he writes, "and then, relax completely; fall back as if you will be caught. Ask! We are no different, you and me. What you ask for you receive."

The words leap off the page. Truth feels soft and calming. Yet, the persona voice speaks up oozing with it's snide sneer; "Well, if that isn't ridiculous. If that isn't pie in the sky, and just plain absurd. Ask Jesus to come! Absurd."

Absurd. The word itself draws me in. It continues to flutter, a gaudy falcon, as I sit. The whole morning feels as absurd as Sister Corita painting the sky with love and her name, leaving huge colors on oil tanks all over the northeast.

Yet? Yogananda spoke truth so clearly. He said over and over, "The Divine has a plan and it is beautiful. Ask Jesus to come to you," He spoke with authority and with power. I admire him partially because he did not equivocate.

So it is on this day, in an insane world, that this fierce absurdity flies right into my heart. I sit for a long time mulling, pondering. I see how I have felt that I must somehow be perfect, be different than I am, to be acceptable to this God One. Why would Jesus talk to someone like me?

Yet? Is it possible? And what would it look like? I take it as a kind of challenge. After all, all souls are equal. Why not?

I mean, why not? What is there to lose? I tell my truth; life has been a challenge lately.

I relax completely and I let go. Then, I ask; I ask for Jesus to come. "Some help is needed here." I ask from the place of hoping I am heard. Knowing I am not perfect and that on the whole, I like where I am. Yes, life is mainly good. I ask for guidance. I ask for Jesus again. Let's have a chat, okay?

Asking and then stillness. Forty or so minutes later and I fall into a light-filled space. Blissful waves play and pulsate through me, lift me up. Sounds of wind and ocean flow through and take me deeper; listening draws inward. Sounds surround and move through this empty body. Then, the world drops away. No body, no mind and thoughts at a great distance.

Awarenesses comes. "Love all my children." And, "Don't look for love out there; they are merely trying to survive. Come here, within." An image of my family twinkles and is gone. And, "Know that it's all perfect." Timeless, swimming in luminescence. Above all, the deep feeling of being held, revered, embraced by love that is light in this no time and no space. Melted.

Then, a sound on the edges, a knocking. Then someone calling. More knocking. The body feels stiff and strange. My carpenter friend, who is building a small deck on my cottage knocks. Damn. I think it has been maybe twenty minutes. I wobble to the door, glance at the clock, which says it has been almost five hours since I sat. Since I asked.

Timeless. I let him in and disappear into the forest to sit. To cry. A death. I see clearly that the experience of having died is part of this. For so long this niggling feeling of dying young had run my life. Little did I know that falling out of the ego feels like a death! AFLO (Yes, another fecking learning opportunity.) Perhaps some of the masks of being this or that were shaken off. Maybe. I don't know anything.

So, a glimpse. On the one hand I feel chosen and on the other? It must be some kind of mistake. I wasn't worthy, not ready. Exactly that. For here I am back in the body, singing alone to the pond.

The next morning I breathe through the exact same yoga asanas I had done the day before; only this time I throw in a head stand. Sky at my feet, the pond on my face, geese laughing and flapping. Once again I sit. Peace. The light returns. Then tears. At the end I give thanks, and more, always and always, more thanks.

I had asked and been given. For me it seemed simple. Easier than algebra, almost like geometry. Yet, now I feel as if I must tell the world. Tell without words, for what is there to say? I am suddenly tired of being alone.

Grace speaks. By grace I was given a glimpse of my own deepest Self. The persona "me" disappeared. A true knowing of immortality or eternity, yes, timelessness seemed to expand the soul. Afterwards, a gratitude filled me up. Grace had brought me into this Holy Arising. Grace - the power of love that penetrates illusion. Grace - the power inside love. Most of us have been touched by it. It changes things. Grace. What a universe.

*

Just Ask

I had asked. There had been no magical techniques, no rites or prayer, no one telling me I was guilty, nothing but dropping deeper into this field of shimmering Presence. The paradox of spirit. Here and not here. Yet, I had relaxed deeply. No matter that I was feeling frustrated or demanding. No matter that I had bouts of sadness, rage, hatred of the world. These feelings come and go; the Infinite holds them as they come. And as they go, I wanted the love of the Divine. As much as I had yearned, THAT wanted me even more.

This field of shimmering grace is a magnet. As you turn inward and relax, as you come to see through the heart, delight in your innocence, all is given. What time is it? Time for another big cosmic laugh.

The Cosmic Joke

Mystic experiences remind me that this world is truly a place of wonder and humility. I also began to see that we can live in our beingness all the time not just when sitting in Presence. This shimmering Presence, this pure 'being aware of being aware,' is who we are in truth. Out of this I felt a deep releasing of who I thought I was. An inner and unshakeable peace. Yes, I still felt anger and frustration but as I breathed with every feeling I embraced it within this larger embrace of trust and acceptance.

These mystic experiences came and went but they were for me signposts that kept me alert. They pointed to other dimensions. They pointed to Reality beneath the appearances of the world. Love flowed through. Grace. I see and sense this love often as it streams from the eyes and hearts of others.

For a few?

This awakening from the dream is a part of every culture and is in in the literature of all cultures. It is not only for the saints, yogis, rishis and shamans but for ordinary folk in every country of the world.

The masters and bodhisattvas call it cosmic conscious - ness; the Mystic Christians, the Holy Instant or the *unio Mystica*. Yogananda calls it, "Self-realization and God consciousness." Some call it a "peak experience" some call it "coming home." It is not something "other worldly" but grounded in our own true nature right here and right now.

Reflect on this. right here and right now.

Edgar Mitchell, the astronaut, experienced it as a "blinding epiphany of meaning," a sense of the perfection of the universe and the natural intelligence of the cosmos which held him and all in perfect alignment. His life was never the same.

Perfect alignment. It was so like the Aramaic "attunement" to the Lord, asked for by Jesus' friends/disciples, which called forth the Prayer to the Lord.

In truth? We are all remembering that we are already one with this Infinite Beingness. A verb rather than a noun. And yet? Words can but point to this wondrous Reality. It is not other worldly but right here and now. We unfolded out of this; it is our real parents! That is why Jeshua called it Abba or Mother/Father God.

All share a sense of timelessness, and being part of "a seamless whole," as William James describes it. The ineffable joy and peace that it leaves and which seems beyond description is shared by all who heed their deeper call.

The call to come home.

Pondering:

I bless all my creations. Sit after a breath; see what comes into your awareness. Something you had a regret about, a person you judged or treated without respect. Ask forgiveness. Know that at the level of soul that person hears you. Bless them: "I bless you with the love of the divine I AM. With the love of the Christ I AM."

Forgive me, I am sorry.
Thank you. I love you.

When I could not forgive my father it was like being dead while still moving about, simply going through the motions.

To forgive is an ongoing practice that finally banishes the cobwebs in the heart. Who do you choose to forgive right now? Is there someone you ask to forgive you? Ask it as a wonder question, ask it within. Wait and see whose face or voice appears. At times i simply forgive everyone, from all lifetimes, who hurt me or abandoned me. And I ask all to forgive me for whatever hurt I gave without knowing. IN truth? only the persona feels hurt.

memoir - Forgiveness, letting go of Guilt

I share this from my devoted friend, David Shepler. -EB

No more that 75 feet ahead, hidden behind another vehicle, an oncoming black F350 Ford truck with a massive chrome grill suddenly swerved into our lane. With less than half a second to respond, there was no chance of avoiding fate. The 100 mph impact between the two vehicles demolished the front end of our car, tearing away the driver's side wheel, roof pillar and door and wracking the entire vehicle.

When the mist cleared, I beheld my beloved wife dangling listlessly from the car's gaping wound, restrained only by the driver's seat belt.

Extricating myself from the wreck and crouching on my knees beside her, blood pumped from her nostrils and mouth. A steady stream. I knew immediately there was no chance of saving her. All I could do was to hold her head up tenderly in my hands, blood pooling in my palms, and tell her over and over how deeply I loved her, whispering to her as she took her last breath, "I shall love you for all eternity. We shall always be One".

And when her eyes glazed over, I felt my heart freeze.

Reflected in myriad fragments of fractured windshield littering the black asphalt canvass, the landscape of my life lay shattered before me. Half my life I had searched the world, remembering her from the past- the many lifetimes we had journeyed together. She was my true reflection, my twin-soul. Consummate heartbreak, the extreme violence of her death had torn open a deep primordial wound, the illusion of separation from Spirit.

Approaching from behind, a man inquired about her condition. "She's passed on," I replied evenly in disbelief, as if witnessing a dream that wasn't really real, a nightmare that wasn't meant to be. An awkward silence settled over us. Stating that the vehicle in front of him had jammed on its brakes, the man mumbled apologetically that he had tried to avoid hitting the trailer he had been following. I felt a wave of anguish and remorse wash over him as he stood behind me.

Moments later he wandered aimlessly away...

~ ~ ~

Adding insult to injury, twice victimized, for two and a half years my step daughters and I have been held hostage to the predictable chess game between insurance companies and lawyers. An undisputed case of wrongful death, there is no compassion in this contest, only the interests of gamblers and opportunists looking to take advantage.

There has been no contact between the Defendant and myself since the incident, save a note I left in his mailbox some time ago. Sensing that he carried a heavy burden of remorse, as a gesture of goodwill, I offered to meet with him personally were it to ease his heart to express his feelings about the incident. I concluded by stating that I hoped whatever settlement was reached might serve to be a healing resolution for both of us. Though the offer had apparently appealed to him, his insurance lawyer expectedly nixed it.

Mediation scheduled for today, I have again proposed meeting with the Defendant personally before the insurance company and lawyers set the tone negotiating a potential settlement. To make it more comfortable for him to meet face to face, I have suggested that the mediator be present simply as a witness while John and I get to know each other a bit, hopefully allowing for compassion and forgiveness to find a place. Surprisingly, the lawyers have obliged.

As John takes a seat across the conference table from me, I note that his health has declined since the accident. A handsome man for sixty-plus years of age, his face has become gaunt and sallow. I have been told beforehand that he has health issues and has been battling throat cancer. Confronted with mortality on three fronts, his wife is said to have Multiple Sclerosis. He tells me about their relationship, a second marriage, and his fondness for her and her family. The depth of his devotion is palpable. Clearly this man has a good heart; and I can't help but feel his anguish and pain. Although different, it may well be as profound as mine.

I begin by stating, "I have wanted to meet with you personally, John, that we might have an opportunity to speak heart to heart. It may seem surprising, but I have never felt ill-will towards you."

He receives this statement with gratitude and grace, addressing me respectfully as "Sir", a formality that appears to be his habitual manner with strangers. "A day hasn't gone by that I haven't been haunted by what happened... If I'd had the sense to stop for a break, gotten something to eat, I wouldn't have been as tired..." His voice trails off, tears stain his face.

To make conversation, I inquire about his property in Vermont, which has recently been listed for sale. It's a beautifully landscaped property with labyrinthian lagoons in open lands and a contemporary home secluded in woodlands, accessed by a long meandering serpentine drive. He replies that his passion is gardening and that the fields were swampland when they bought the property. Complimenting him, I suggest that he is a natural geomancer and that we have this passion in common: a love of the land and co-creating with Nature.

After some back and forth, I tell him that I feel compassion and forgiveness for him, and that I hope that it will help him to find forgiveness for himself. "We're humans, John, we make mistakes. Learning from one's mistakes one is absolved. No blame. My wife is present here with us in spirit now. She want's me to convey to you that we bear no judgement…"

As we part company turning to settlement negotiations, I wonder: how would it feel to be in this man's place? The guilt, the shame, the remorse for the loss of another's life? Might John's experience be as anguishing as mine? More difficult, perhaps, to move beyond without resorting to denial?

The human soul is burdened by subconscious guilt. Hidden existential guilt. Its roots are primordial: the fall from Grace and the knowledge of one's true Divine Nature. It presents itself in life in endless guises. Such as accidents. Spiritually linked by tragedy, how can I not feel compassion for this man's suffering, being a reflection of my own? Forgiveness: is this not ultimately about forgiving oneself?

-David Shepler, 2016

The Greatest Miracle

Some believe they must travel to meet a teacher of miracles. I did this and I found the teacher merely pointed to my heart. "Be here," she said. "If you are worried or angry you cannot be here." I was perplexed.

Was this the greatest miracle?

There was a way -shower who breathed with me and as I began to truly allow the breath, my body was illuminated. He said, "Allow all to be as it is." When the breathing is jagged, I find only illusion of past and future. When the breath is shallow I find only resentment and judgement. If I have not forgiven another or myself, it is hard to breathe; without the breath I could not know the peace which pervades all that is.

As I travelled I remembered that the greatest miracle does not lie in the mountains or in the sea. It does not lie in the beauty of another or in a work of art; for in truth they lie in it. *All is held in this shining Self.* This shining sea of awareness. For the greatest miracle lies in this life, knowing we are held and we are an offspring of this pure awareness. Truth is beauty is knowing and is the greatest miracle.

When I return to the heart I return to the silence from which all sound comes. All creation comes from sound; it is all vibration. It is pure light. Even thoughts which come and go are vibrations. As I breathe I fall into the heart. Fall into stillness. As my teacher said to me, "Join with me, here in the heart." So I say to you, "meet me here."

For beneath this thinking mind is the mystery. Some call this loving essence God or Infinite One; some say pure awareness. I know only this, Love is. Here there is no confusion. Here there is no conflict or resentment. Here there is no judgment. This Pure Self is the Shimmering presence of God. There is no-thing here. This is the greatest gift. The greatest miracle. Abide in the Heart and know the silence. Be still.

All Creation is equal. This is the great truth; and it is anathema to the ego which seeks specialness, which seeks contrast, which seeks hierarchy. which wants power and control – so it can stay in control. And never know peace.

Each expression of the One is unique.

You are, an offshoot of the Infinite;
  you are perfect,
    innocent and
      eternal.

Ponder this.

I sit on a deck over the Pond. I swim and then move onto my yoga mat. This energy moving through the body still feels wondrous. After loves breath, I sit. Stillness. When I move out of the mind into the sensations and the breath, I feel a kind of shimmering throughout the body.

It is as if I have come out of some dream.

I had fallen into the field. Some call it the Infinite field. The persona mind stepped aside, and I experienced Christ consciousness. Or Buddha consciousness and the zero point field or nirvana; what matters words? The dream of separation disappeared. Expecting more peace on this day, I am attentive to a tightness erupting through me.

At first it feels like a tension in the throat but soon it strangles and feels unbearable. My heart feels suffocated, my head is swirling with vertigo, and my throat is congested and closing off. I want to see it as an allergic reaction. "Good," I say, "let's play some music, take an allermax and bypass the whole thing."

But I don't. I just sit. Now? I know better. The Way of Mastery is a great teacher.

It feels like a fire in my bones, then a loneliness. An image comes; I see myself as a child, coming into this world with love and open arms. I see how my enthusiasm, my screaming with joy, my running through the house, upsets the parents. Spanked, yelled at, locked in a room until my joy turned to anger subsides, I feel shut down. The old feeling of being squashed, alone, with no one listening.

Hopelessness. I want to hate them but that does not happen. So I turn the hate inward onto myself. Yes, bad, I must be bad. If I rebel too loudly they may refuse to feed me. They are all I know of God. As a child, my image of God comes from them. They are my protectors and caretakers. They are my first entrance into the world; their loving touch, their caring vibration is a mirror for who I believe I am as I grow.

I stop breathing; the loneliness subsides. Breathing again and now and my heart feels suffocated. I know the feeling will go away if I eat or do something. So, instead of cleaning the bathroom, I sit.

Soon, in an astounding turn, I feel it color the sky, the water, the geese who come each year to show off their young. Now? Everything surrounding me is in misery. Surely this misery comes from outside of me? But as I breathe more deeply I see how my feelings project onto this "world" that seems to be outside of me; but is not. I am the one coloring this neutral event, this wholly innocent and placid arising of light and shadow. I project the world and I have changed it into a world filled with melancholy.

For four hours I sit, breathe and allow this old sadness to deepen. If the sadness turns, I go into the forest and let myself rage to the trees for five or ten minutes. The trees take it in. You can take feelings to the trees. I howl. The trees hold me, the sky becomes my mother. I continue and become raw. I feel naked and vulnerable, just a plate of nerve endings without my beliefs or thoughts to hide behind.

This deep sadness is brought into the light. These feelings are energies that need to move through the body like rain and windstorms move through the earth. And? I begin to enjoy allowing them. Yes, an enjoyment based on feeling and opening completely. For months afterwards I take my feelings here, to the trees. I sit and allow.

Who is it that knows of this sadness? Who is it that experiences loneliness? A wonder question of great fruit.

Later, I can call it something - the alchemy of sounding. This gives it some status. Allowing sounds to carry the feelings. Really, it is just allowing what has been stuck in me since childhood. Or? It may not even be mine. I remember that nothing is personal and we are all connected. It may be my Aunt Caroline's sadness that she held onto as she ate more and more to stuff away her loneliness.

I now accept, even trust, these feelings. Grateful, I feel I am found. And? As soon as I feel more whole and calm; I sleep. Then? I enjoy the unexpected. I find that soon I will allow the feelings to run through me, a bit of sound or not, or there will be another wave and I am off again to sit, to feel and express. Nothing is personal in this universe.

Afterwards? I dance. Yes, dance and dance.   -1991

We awaken at our edges. Sound is an alchemy that allows the
flow of feeling. And laughter always follows.

Heaven is spread out over this earth but humankind sees it not. Heaven is a state of Being, a state of deep Presence, not a place. In Reality? Heaven is right where you are. Remember, consciousness has many mansions. Consciousness has many dimensions.

Pondering

When I truly took this breath into the bones of my being, breathed deep into my marrow, I felt a new lightness. An expansion. When you keep your attention inward throughout your day, there is little that can push you off balance.

1. The heart chakra is the center of our being. Through the heart center moves all emotions, thoughts, ideas. The heart chakra is always open,

2. The ego or persona has no real existence. It is a conglomeration of memories, beliefs, thoughts that I call "me." Most people live through the filter of the ego. The ego cannot know the Infinite or bliss or peace. It is a great servant of the heart (the core of our consciousness) but a terrible master. Ego means to edge God out.

3. Gratitude is the attitude of enlightenment. Gratitude for the gift of life and all the gifts of this life helps take the shackles off the heart. As I become the one who brings love, who blesses, I quit looking for approval and love from the world. Gratitude spreads outward into the field. As I bring love to my own being and allow all my feelings to be as they are - expressed, felt, and trusted, the heart opens. Feelings are the road to my wholeness. Allowing them takes care of the inner child who was not allowed to feel all feelings.

WINTER AGAIN

The breath is a portal to this moment Now.

Yet, even this is not completely of truth.

For Now speaks of a then and there is no "then."

There is only this arising.

This arising is a doorway to eternity.

This arising is eternity.

An invitation to surrender is in the breath.

Make your home in the breath

memoir - I first met you Jesus

On the trail of the secret at the heart of the universe,
Everyone will meet Jesus. In a story, a cartoon, a joke,
in the bible or on the road. We met in a basement.   EB

Sullivan's Island, South Carolina 1950

....I first met you Jesus, while you were hanging by one tack off the mildewed walls of a church basement. Sunday school, then, was always held in cold, musty concrete basements with chipped floors, an upright piano and posters partially hung from weary masking tape.

It's a real meeting without intermediaries. I meet you while the teacher isn't looking. Your eyes are deep and welcoming. Everyone else is sitting at the long table waiting for Mrs. Knitter to hand them paper, gold stars and finger paints. We are all around four or five years of age and impressed by everything shiny and just out of reach.

You are tall, dark skinned with liquid hazel eyes, a well-kept curly reddish brown beard and long wavy hair. You remind me of a Breck shampoo girl with that shimmering hair. From your heart there is a light streaming. That light is even coming from the sun over your left shoulder. Sucking up your sun, I am biting my lip and I am not alone. You are surrounded by children sitting among daisies and poppies gazing at you with smiles only ice cream brings.

I know why. Yes, I know. It's your hands; they are raised up. They are ready. Ready to fly and waiting in the rapt anticipation of an event of import, of awe-striking wonder and upliftment. Yes, oh, and all of creation is waiting for that downbeat to start it all rolling. Once again. A song.

The children are waiting too. I feel right at home. I know how it is, those hands of yours. My grandmother raises hers in the same gesture when she stands before her choir. You are paused between verses and the look on the children's faces is the same as theirs; eyebrows raised, eyes stone open, tongues wetting lips. Everyone as still as rocks, but with all cells and atoms on the lip of ecstasy. I know it all. You aren't a foreigner to me, you are one of us. Like Geneva you are a conductor. Ready, mark and here it comes!. Like Rosa, your hands are poised as a hundred voices flow and wash over the mountains and lakes. Over the earth. Into my bones and through the intricate wood and bone of the most holy piano.

*

The children in the poster are paused too, waiting for the downbeat. It raced my heart. Above it all? Birds are flying, clouds hovering and your robes glisten with a laser light that comes out of your heart. I know that heart light, I know it well. Who doesn't know about Cupid?

While the second Sunday school teacher, Miss Evelyn, round-faced and earnest, fumbles with buttons, glue, scissors, the glaring eyes of the little boys, I bask in the glory of your kinetic love song. That song which is about to begin. Anticipation. Just about there. The downbeat held back. The promise of love. The almost taste of ice cream. The yearning before the birthday party. Waiting for the magic kiss, the magic red shoes. I sit on edge. I pull up a chair. Front row seat. Feet flat on the concrete. This is not going to be missed.

*

Your name, Jesus, had been heard many times before, as Miss Knitter talked.

"Everyone should be like Jesus, loving and accepting and always seeing the good in everyone," Ya, yah, yah, while the boys made faces.

"If we were," she burbled, "then the world would be a heaven on earth."

Double yawn, ya, ya, ya.

Yet, what I remember from that time of sitting with you? On the faces of your children is raw and unbridled enthusiasm, and pure, oh, what can only be summed up in one word. Joy.

You were a star, yet, the whole picture raised some questions in my pre-pondering state. For one, if following your example was the purpose, then, why weren't we singing? Class closed with a prayer both lackluster and hurried compared to what your children are about to sing. I knew then, that you and the children, why they could make the spine tingle. It looked like four part harmony and I heard oboes, harps, bells, and maybe a triangle gleaming. Snuffling through something on being righteous, well, what did that have to do with the heavenly singing and heartlights streaming I saw before me?

It wasn't enough. Neither was it enough when I looked around at all the church people as they came out of the big hall; there were the anxious faces above gray suits that hung worried over ties dark and tight holding it altogether. Something was amiss. I didn't know what.

*

My country grandmother, Geneva, was Baptist and was Choir director at the Reformed Presbyterian Church. When she raised her hands a torrent of unexpected sounds poured out of the faces of bemused and quite ordinary folk. She loved church music and occasionally took me to Baptist African American

211

churches to hear the singing and the sermon. Baptist churches exploded with high frequency music and people bursting with the good news. The jiving bodies, at times, raised her fine nose high but the gospel and hymns brought up tears.

*

In my room with my small radio, I followed the popular music and sang along. Later, I played piano-Chopin, Debussy, Mozart jazz, folksongs and sang along. Sounds and singing led to devotional prayer and mantra. This devotional way of India and eastern cultures brings us into immediate connection with our heart and therefore the Infinite Self. Do you see?

Mantras connect me to the heart. Sounds create this universe and we are vibrational beings. The power of Mantra, of singing sounds has been a part of ancient cultures - part of their ways of connecting to the Creator, to nature, to each other. Nature is alive with sound and the simple joy of being alive! We see it in all that flutters and flies and digs and runs. Who is the listening one, the seed of stillness from which all sound, spirit, for arises.

Close the eyes. Hum and then sing the AUM or simply speak the words of a loving mantra: Loka Samasta Sukino, Bhavantu.

Then? Be the stillness. Sound arises from the silence returning therein.

Breathlight

Feel into how the breath breathes you. Take three long breaths that
begin in the belly; let the attention and energy end down in the
solar plexus. Feel the body as a hollow luminous flute in which the
light of breath easily moves.

Notice the sense of existing. The realization of beingness; be one
with this space in which all arises - sounds, thoughts, the body,
trees, houses.
Let go of these objects. Be one with the space.

Bring attention only to the BEING which is the space in which all
arises. Listen for the sounds around you. Notice the senses are
sensing perfectly - without any effort from you.
Be one with the spaciousness. No imagining or creating.

The crown chakra is open. Feel light pouring into the crown.
Allow the light to move through into the heart which is simply
light. From there, the lightbreath flows into the spaciousness.
Relax. Sense the Softness. Listen. Listen.

My parents had no religious pictures of any kind, and though my mother took us to church every Sunday, my father stopped going when I was seven. He was angry as a boiled owl about church people and had forsworn all church going forever. He denounced it as a place for those who were "saints on Sundays and thieves and pagans the rest of the time." As a moral man he knew he knew the difference.

Yet, at the end of his life, his body twisted and drenched in pain, he didn't want to leave and he cried out, "I've been bad. I am going to hell. God will judge me. I was so, so bad."

His hands gnarled and clasped on hard to the bed metal. White knuckled he was holding even harder onto the belief that he was bad, bad, bad. So bad that no one could help him. He had waited too late to turn it all around. Baptist sermons were filled with hellfire from the evangelists of his day. Crying out from the circle of sinners he knew that he was guilty. And if you feel guilty, well, it follows that you must have done something so dirty down clap your belly bad-wrong and beyond all mercy and salvation.

"Dad?" I had to yell to get his attention as he was gasping while ripping his hospital robe into tatters. "THIS has been hell. Right here on earth. Remember all those days of struggling, of not getting a pension or retirement, seeing how Mom cried at yet another move across the country? That was not Heaven exactly. But it was okay, wasn't it okay?"

Briefly, he eyed me.

"Dad, believe me, you are now going to heaven. You are not going to be judged. And," I added in my lower than low alto voice, "you haven't done anything wrong…"

"What in the name of Jeesus, do you know?" He yelled back at me. "About anything?"

"Dad! Dad, I know one thing is that, really and truly, I am going to miss you.."

"What?" He yelled. "What's the issue?"

Blank and empty of rhetoric on that day, I gave up all but blessing him. I trust he hears me somewhere in that scared and lonely place inside his head where he hangs out.

Then, of course, what did I know? I was leading from my own confusion. Numerous times we had this strained conversation; from college I brought home all my newly acquired wisdom and laid it on his table. He played kickball with just about everything that excited me. He could kick my passions over a mile.

The day before the night he let himself go, I told my father about Jesus and how I had first met him. "Jesus loves singing, and children and, well, Dad, you two have a lot in common." A strange thing to say, even for me. But here he was at the last station before the last train pulled out and I was chewing hard on how to rally his focus.

"Dad, listen now, remember how you could burst out into "Oh My Papa," and "Somewhere over the Rainbow," while you were shaving or washing your latest most favorite car?"

He turned, silent, nostrils trembling, drenched with sweat and tears, regarding me from swollen eyes and a face misery. "Dad, you and Jesus? You both love singing."

His memory was tentative along with his self-forgiveness and he was sure he was unsalvageable. Right rather than happy was his mantra. His great sense of humor and love of laughter had fled the room. Who was I to shake his unshakeable beliefs?

That night when he finally let go he was berating himself and rehashing his huge regrets. He was calling up his mother Geneva who had first overstuffed his fat cells with too many grits. It may seem a small regret, but on that bed of leaving, unless we have become conscious of our blames and lack of forgiveness, those small seemingly petty angers may rise up once again. And knock us between the eyes.

Haunted by the vision of quick wealth, no matter what he made, it was never enough. And that was the follow-up to the deep program that he was never enough, those two being twins in the fantasy world of his conjuring. Tightly wound, his whole body grimaced in an iron corset of fear, he held onto those regrets, the self-hating judgements until, deep in the night, he let go. I heard it second -hand, for In his room was an angel of leaving; Ruby. An imposing round-eyed Black woman, she related, how it all came to pass. Hands folded, she prays for a white man she knew only in his leaving days. "You know,"she said, "it was his fingers went first. Then his crying. Then? The Lord done made him peaceful and I sang him a lullaby as he went out."

He gave up. No more trying for control of life. No more trying to be a captain of media. His face seamless, his hands nestled together; his body sinking back into the elements, I saw him as perfect, as innocent, once again and ready to be borne even into the fire. I ask that he comes across you, Jesus, and that circle of children. That he be invited to sing alto and teach them a few songs that only the Andrew Sisters and Frank Sinatra know how to sing. All things, with prayer and infinite patience, come to pass. May you walk on heavenly meadows and swim in peaceful water.

-EB 2000

Mystics and Physicists

Physicists and Mystics: the meeting

To me, science is one way of connecting with the mystery of existence. I'm talking about science as part of a much grander and older sort of questioning about who we are in the big picture of the universe…. science really becomes a deeply spiritual conversation with the mysterious, about all the things we don't know.

-Marcelo Gleiser, theoretical Physicist at Dartmouth College.

Mystics and Physicists Meet

In Presence, in meditation, we relax into our true nature.. It is not something we do, but it is the truth of who we are - beingness. It is our Reality.

The world lives by certain beliefs it presumes to be true. As we know beliefs are changeable. At one time we knew for sure that the earth is the center of the galaxy, that the sun circles around the earth and that the earth is flat. So much for beliefs.

My early Yoga experiences and readings included this phrase: "We float in a sea of consciousness." The Mystic Christ path elucidates the same knowing. The Sufis holds the same knowing. Until I relaxed into the felt realization of this, it was just another belief. The Truth of the Infinite is in relaxing into Presence. Trusting all as it is. Experience, not belief, has been my mantra.

-The world culture and science present the belief that consciousness came after creation and arose from matter, even arose from the human brain at some point in human history. This would mean that awareness is limited in each person.

- Now, Quantum Physics challenges this and is questioning many presumptions previously taken as truth. I put my faith in my own experience. So it is with many of the Yogis, Seers and Shamans.

In Yoga class we play with the experience of the body and have found that our awareness is not limited, does not stop at the skin of the body.

You must experience it for yourself.

The question must come up: How can consciousness be derived from matter?

The mind's interpretations are not the experience itself.

*

This quantum field is being revealed by not only Quantum Physicists but by all those desiring radiant health. Acupuncture, Tai Chi, Yoga, Jin Shin Jyutsu, reiki, Reconnective Healing, all help restore your unique flow and allow your natural energy patterns to realign with this field.

This ancient truth is known by all sages and masters. The conscious energetic field includes layers of energies, which interpenetrate each other; it is affected by our choices, actions, thoughts and emotions. It is also affected by our breathing patterns.

The very same dynamic is also true for the planet earth. The balance and specific health of her atmosphere determines the health of her physical manifestation. Since all is bathed in the same field of pure consciousness, it is time to bring our attention to this pure knowing. This is what it means to incarnate. this is what is meant by Reality.

The Meeting.

The thing is that the world is in a constant state of motion; and there is nothing of matter in it; just these ever changing patterns of dancing photons in an infinite field of possibilities.

*

Newton described a material world in which individual particles of matter followed certain laws of motion through space and time – the universe as machine.

*

Physics has revealed that at the subatomic level, the objects we encounter in the world dissolve into 'particles' and 'waves' that can only loosely be said to have shape and form or even mass.

*

According to quantum physics, objects are possibility waves, called wave-functions. Particle physics states that matter is not a fundamental property of physics. There aren't two fundamental physical entities, but only one: Energy/ waves of probability

*

There is nothing set or predictable. And here is the wonderment1 The observer actually changes what is being observed. The intention and deep desire of the observer will bring about varied and unique outcomes.

*

221

The Universe is Light

The entire universe(s) is (are) made up of photons of light and information, a matrix of infinite possibilities. This matrix has no properties apart from what we do with it. Our intention to allow change enters into a dance in which change happens.

*

By looking out at the seeming physical/energy world scientists are finding out what the rishis, yogis, prophets, yogis, masters and shamans know from looking within. The outer world and the inner world are being seen in truth as one luminous web of Pure Light which is pure Consciousness.

*

Masters from all spiritual traditions call what happens, miracles. Physicists call what happens, potentialities.
All is Holy, all is Sacred. All is the One.

*

All is connected, all is one ocean of light. Further, science has found that the universe is a fractal universe. This means that in each fragment is found the whole. Mystics have always said, "Within you is the entire universe. Sit. Be still. Let the mind fade into the background. There is nothing to fear."

*

As in all else, you must experience it for yourself. This Light is pure consciousness. I experience it as pure Love.

*

Zero Point Field

After freezing matter to a point in which all of it ceases to move, there is still this shimmering vibration. Quantum Physicists call this the Zero Point Field. It is the living matrix, intelligent and alive, and in which all is birthed in all moments. Many have called it the unified field that Einstein searched for; many wonder if it is pure consciousness, a light so refined it cannot be quantified, and yet is the ocean out of which all is born.

The Vedas, the ancient books from India, describe it this way, "The essence of God is always right here and right now; its center is everywhere its circumference cannot be found. And it is utter mystery. You cannot analyze it, yet, you can melt into it. As pure awareness it is the ocean in which we float. This Presence is everywhere equally."

So many names

Source, Abba (Mother/Father God) Consciousness, Being, Amma/Divine Mother, Abhwoon, the Field, the primordial spiral, Light, the logos, the jewels of Indra, the AUM, God, the I AM, Lord and Beloved.

Different names for the same Field of creation. Given this, how can anyone call it theirs? Or give it a label? We are all the dancing offspring children of this pure unfolding pulsating dance of creation.

Breathe.

Love is the very nature of Being itself. We live in this field of God. God is "the one in whom we live, move, and have our being."

"Playing in the fields of the Lord." Does this not take on a grand meaning? The word "Lord" in Aramaic means "Shimmering Presence of Loving Oneness." Are we not all playing in this field of Self? This field of pure loving awareness?

The yogis call it the dance of Shiva/Shakti. Out of the unmanifest consciousness of Shiva, pure stillness, comes the dancing forms of Shakti. It is the Creator expressing itself through creation. The Divine Mother, then, is this unfolding, expanding universe in which all forms dance into being and back into pure spirit.

What is a master?

A master is the perfect student.

A master steps into the moment without beliefs or ideas,
without judgments or opinions. Knowing that all is perfect
and allowing all to be as it is.

(S)he enters the moment with the curiosity and innocence
of a child. At peace and knowing that she is pure awareness and
always one with that which birthed her; with that which is the field
of beingness.

For creation is new and ever new again.
As is the soul.

What does it mean to live as a master?
It means before everything, to take a deep breath. With
whatever is arising, whatever is happening, before all else,
breathe. This creates a gap, a space in which you may choose
how to respond. To choose anew to come from fear or acceptance
and trust.
It means to resist nothing.

Pondering

Q: What is a belief?

A: 'To fervently wish that something is true.'

And, 'A thought that you keep on thinking.'
Ponder this.

In belief the mind holds a position without proof. The mind is not in a relaxed knowing state of peace, allowance, Presence. The mind 'charges' this thought with emotion in the hope of generating the power to make it real, and to defend it against an 'assault.' This is because to mind, this belief is desperately needed.[39]

When people in this charged state feeling only the rightness of their beliefs come together there is conflict. Belittling, anger, killing, pushing apart or separation and war may follow. We all know this program. There is another program before it:

"I would rather be right than in peace." Or "I would rather be right than in joy or live in harmony."

Light Beings

We are light beings. Our energy field influences the entire field of the Infinite. We are creators. We anchor divine consciousness into this Reality and dimension through our willingness, our allowing and our inviting. Scientists know that our cells give off light. We are truly bio-photonic beings.

Q: How do I nurture and strengthen my light body?

A: First, acknowledge and honor who you are. "I am awake and fully embodied. I am anchored to the earth. I am one with Infinite Spirit. I am one with the Father/Mother God."

Second, know that we are floating in this field of pure light/awareness. Feel, sense and allow the light to flow through your crown chakra, through the body, and into the earth. Realize how the breath floods your cells with light which is life force (prana).

Breathe in the light of nature.

As you take a walk reach out and gather the life energy of trees. Appreciate nature; the animals the plants, the water, the earth. Sound harmonizes the light body. Play music that you love.

Allow the light to enter at the crown chakra. Imagine the sunlight entering your body. At first you imagine; then you begin to feel it flowing through you.

"Until we extend our circle of compassion to all living things, humanity will not find peace."
-Albert Schweitzer

Why? Because there is only one light, yet many forms.

Pondering:

If what is real is real forever and if what is true is true eternally, and I promise you it is so, then ask the Wonder question:

Q: *What is it that is eternal about me?*

As you sit, bring your attention to your fingers. Attention is an ability or extension of awareness. Now feel your toes. Now, look at something in the room - the window or door. Bring your attention back to the body bring it to the belly, solar plexus, torso. Feel your sense of beingness. As empty.

What is it that is aware of being aware?
Notice: you are now aware of your awareness.

Withdraw your attention from the objects of awareness; be aware only of awareness itself. Does it have boundaries? The edge of the skin? Be still and feel into it. It is important to simply experience this and not go into the little persona mind for interpretation.

"Enlightenment; It is an art and a science."   *-Swami Yogananda*

Cosmic consciousness is our true and natural state of being.
this other living from the ego is abnormal and dysfunctional.

The Shimmering field in which all is illuminated

One thing for sure? When we know our True Self, the nature of this field of consciousness in which all experience appears, we know that which is the Creator. The mind, body and world may then become transparent to us. And we see it as it is - a joyous play of light and shadow in the field of pure consciousness. Smile. Breathe. Allow. Surrender.

As you sit and come into feeling-communion with yourself you will experience Truth. You will knowing True knowing. Reality.

Truth

I am nothing and I have nothing....

Yes, the relaxing into what is always here and now is itself exhilarating! It is an enchanted Kingdom to move and breathe and give thanks. And then, truly, some things are best left in the kingdom of the mystery. It is still a mystery as to how and why anything exists at all and why and how awakening can take place. I sit to allow the emptiness.

Grace follows. Of this?

I know nothing

This universe is self-aware.

I relax into this Presence and am aware of this awareness; all else fades and what seemed hidden shines forth.

We are living in a conscious self-aware universe. Few people know this, or will only know this when they leave their bodies.

You can choose to live on the surface of your consciousness, in the persona mind. Or you can choose to wonder, what if? What if Reality is within?

Choose to use time to be in stillness. I chose to be "an experiment of One," as Thoreau said.

Deepen into silence, observe how the persona mind works.

Discover the stillness; it is not within you. It IS you!

Your True Self.

Once you have asked and answered the call?

The end is perfectly certain.

Silence is is a profound melody for those who can hear it above all the noise.   *-Socrates*

Memoir - Crane Girl

Crane girl and the Tree.
Great desire, like for enlightenment, or to bring
heaven on earth, leads you to great expansion.
-Mirabai Devi

A young girl from a village in Korea stands on one leg. Thin, dark, her long hair banded by a white ribbon, she stands in the center of a square. Unchanged for so many years now; the bodies, the blood, the thin girl on one leg.

She stands in the photo which hangs on the southwest wall in my room. She stands beside a tomb of glass which holds two butterflies and a Morpho moth, whose wings shimmer from purple to blue, depending upon the angle of the light. As I have grown older I have changed my angle to the sun. Virginia Wolf may have said it first. If so, I have grown into this knowing.

She hung as the Cranegirl, on my wall, for twenty years. She could have been a dancer, or a gymnast had the photograph not been in a popular magazine from the seventies. The caption reads, "…Chinese soldiers, during a rebellion in Korea, had taken her village over and her parents and brother had been killed. Their bodies lay in the background. Around her the other villagers mourn and keen over the dead. Some cleaned up the debris, washed their brothers and sisters and sat in the streets on their knees as they cried and wiped their noses. She chose to stand."

In the center of the village square she stood on one leg with her hands in namaste at her chest. Her head bent forward and her eyes closed. It is said that she stood that way for twelve hours without moving. She balanced into an

232

unshakeable tranquility. The stillness grew around her; did she become invulnerable? What would she answer?

So I ask her, "Why are you doing this? Don't you see that the others need you? They need you to cook food, to clean, to learn to shoot so this won't happen again. To raise babies and act your age. Don't you see this?"

As I continue I realize I am asking myself these same questions. These are the questions my parents asked me when I chose to teach Yoga, which was, to them, of little use in a material world.

Crane girl does not look up. There is an imperceptible flicker around her wrists; perhaps it is the malaria in the blood pulsing. Her standing foot is purple and tense and twitches to deflect a fly which walks over her skin as if she were a cane of brown sugar. I walk around her, trying to make her look up. She is immoveable yet her body sways as if she were a hollow reed or a sedge at the rim of a pond in which snakes and otters play.

"Crane girl! Help me!" A woman screams.

"Let the dead bury their dead…."

Who said that? I look but her lips are still. A mole rests on the slight indent of her cheek and her forehead is mottled with red and white sun spots. Then? I stand beside her and plant my foot deeper into the sod. I bring my left foot onto my thigh and push and yes, there is balance. Still, it is a constant adjustment. I bend my head slightly and close my eyes. I feel a slight breeze and the earth's vibration gently holding my foot. That is all.

*

233

She is my mythic warrior. Still, she raises my curiosity. I say to her; what do you see within? Why do you not run for cover? You look as though you have found the answer. So I ask you again, tell me, tell us all, what do you see?" Silence. "Are you not caught between two worlds even now? It must be a shaky threshold on which to stand, between two worlds, each with a different definition of virtue."

"Crane girl, I need water. Where is the water?" A bent man sits down at a distance and becomes silent.

"Yes, they define virtue in different ways." Her voice is soft and comes from somewhere around her. *"I questioned. My father was a farmer. He believed in the ancestors. He believed in the village. He believed that one should give up one's life for the leaders, the village, the family. Now he is gone. I do not believe anything. I look without seeing. I breathe. I stand here awhile."*

And your mother?

"My mother was kind and loving. She said it is enough to be married and to worship the ancestors. To learn to grow and love the food, to learn gratitude in each moment for the blessing of the food and the earth. She said, 'Marry and give your body and life over to your husband, your children and the ancestors. It is enough.' With her and with my father I worked in the fields. Now she is gone. My fiancée is gone. All is change. Where is the virtue now? This I ask."

As I do the tree asana, balancing on this crust of earth, meteors fly, waves crash, wars erupt, and all creation turns round and round. Something emerges when I sink down, something lifts me at the elbows. I breathe and give thanks.

234

Now, so many years have gone by and I hear her still. She says it clearly, *"It is enough."*

I know now what words do not touch. It is refusal. It is the refusal to believe as the world believes. It is the refusal to believe in the war that wants to pull her, and all of us, into it's endless vortex. To believe in an unjust war is to become a whore. It may start out as a question, "What should I do now?" But finally, it becomes a stance. For this war rages on through centuries and sets off other wars until everyone is lying bleeding and crying out for help. Or being buried. Or burying their dead. But who wasn't dead once they left their heart for the mind games of revenge?

"No," said the Crane girl.

The article said that the villagers came, one by one, to yell and make faces at her, and then to drop down and sit. Out of exhaustion. Not too close, at a certain distance. For she might be a demon, even now, pretending to be the young girl they knew. Demons can take over bodies. Now she was something else entirely, this stillness. They didn't know how to be with her. So they walked around her. They lay down, they sat. Finally, they are silent.

They would wait. With no reaction, what can be said?

We stand together always, for she is ever here. There is ignorance that must be refused. But then? I return to her. Together in silence and with no interpretation, peace emerges.

She bows deep into the silence. "It is called the Tree," I tell her. "It is a great blessing to all of creation and is given to all humankind. You have become the tree for your people." Refusal and acceptance welded into one.

"Yes," she said to me, "All those who have gone before are with me, circling. It is a crazy dancing circle and they are laughing that I should ever pretend to know suffering."

I am taken by surprise. "The ancestors laughing?"

She rests her hands on her heart. *"Every soul born has a clan of spirits. They always surround you and live in joy."*

"I like this. How can I join you?" I ask her.

"Between the words." she tells me;

"Fall with me just as you dive into a lake. This one-legged dance is just an opening. It is the gentle knocking at the door, do you see?"

Then, she unfolds into the day where she carries water, leads the children in singing and picks and cleans vegetables.

What she poured into me remains. I refuse by the stillness always at the center of my being. The silence holds us in it's loving palm at the end of all seeking. Has she brought heaven to earth? Where is the shelter in words? Where is the light in words? It is best to set your foot steady and make your home in the breath. Here? Find shelter and know the light.

-EB 2008

…There is a cry deeper than all sound
whose serrated edges cut the heart
as we break open to the place inside
which is unbreakable and whole,
while learning to sing.

~~Rashani, Sufi

Intimacy   into -me -see

We are here to celebrate each other. Not to compare
contrast or critique, for this is the ego's world. To simply see that
every creation, every act that is of compassion and love, raises the
frequency of the entire cosmos. You are that powerful.

Pondering:

Wonder beings

We come into this physical realm with all sorts of
abilities and gifts. Intuition, clairvoyance, clairaudience, psychic
powers, ability to leave our body and return at will, healing others
as we allow the flow of the universe to move through us. We are,
in truth, wonder beings.

Yet? Without self-love and acceptance we squander these
gifts wanting to fit in with a world of dramas and approval. And so
we stifle ourselves. These powers or 'siddhis' (Sanskrit) lay
dormant within you. You are now remembering all the profound
gifts that come with self-love and seeing the world as innocent.

The greatness within you cannot be discarded.
It is part of being a divine/human being.

Intuition

> *The intuition is not the equal but rather the superior of all other human faculties.*
> *The greatest power of consciousness is the intuition.* [40]

It is in asking within for help, it is in asking within, "Spirit, what is the context of this event? What am I to learn from this? What is it that best fulfills my highest purpose here and the highest purpose for all creation? For, really, as you attune within, find the stillness and then, allow what arises, there is a still soft voice which makes itself known. Perhaps not right away. Do not rush to find an "answer." Be willing to wait.

> *Only through the pure intuition freed from emotional egoism and transcending intellectual illusion, can one really make a contact with the True Self..and this happens in a state of pure tranquillity.* [41]

memoir - Shimmering Sudsy Bath of Sexy Spirit

It is in this body wherein lies all teachings.
In this body where there is found all suffering,
and in this body where there is found the
end of all suffering.

-The Buddha

Diary, February, 2006

At this moment I am in a bathtub on the top floor of an old mansion in Portland, Oregon. I drink a glass of ginger tea while soap suds are playing with my toes and a song from Rasa flies through. All the while Camellias are blooming through the window.

Ah, the body floats so well.

From here there is only perfection. Skin on skin I embrace myself, use the wash cloth to caress my shoulders which leads to lovely tangs of feeling all over. Skin. It covers up the bones, holds the organs and alerts me to invading bugs, winds, and rain. Mostly, it is a connector to the natural world of creation in which all abides on this giving earth. A transparent membrane, in truth. For as we know it lets in breath and needs to breathe.

Further, skin is a seamless web of bliss, if that is my intention. I am in whole-hearted or holy oneness with this arising and as the water embraces and loves me so I enter the same door, of loving this body and merging with the water. Keep on going, through the next door, of loving the Self. Is this Heaven? Oh, yes. It is my own private paradise. If it is heaven then am I having a spiritual or sexual experience?

This is a question which twenty years ago would have sent me flying into my head to solve. This or that? Then everything was an either/or proposition. Back then I was

240

chastising myself for being a "bad girl," for having too many sensual feelings which I tried in every way to keep under cover. Stuff them back! Meet a few artists, writers and saints, ask for meaning and purpose and guidance and let's get on with it.

Or just leave the body and this world of chaotic relationships, numbed out people, yearnings and sickness behind. Above all keep your sensual stuff (like your money stuff, feeling stuff and your God stuff) a secret. Ola and Zoweee, it does become kind of exhausting, pretending all the time.

There was something about pleasure in the body that sent the culture into a tizzy. Do you notice that? A play with naked people on stage got everyone raging, arguing, writing essays. The answer for most? Sublimate, sublimate, sublimate.

Go build a bridge, become a therapist, talk incessantly, knit miles of scarves, learn Indian cooking, have a child or six or run, run, run. For a few, the answer was live just for the flesh and become a hedonist. Do anything but feel these feelings as heaven sent or as part of this divine play, Lila, on earth.

Because if you're in a spiritual way you must know that nowhere in the bible or in Buddha's literature or in the Gita are you going to find anyone talking about "those" feelings. And here in this culture, women of the night are given dreadful names while randy men are lauded. What's going on here? Could it be that the world is insane? Ah. It is so. Respect and devotion for the feminine seemed of a distant past. There is tantra, but I knew nothing of that then. Religion put a rift between my feelings, my body, my truth, and the Godstream.

Enter a girl named Lucy. She talked to me about Jesus and sex.

241

Raised a Catholic by, as she called them, "unhappy nuns," Lucy was haunted by the cross. The story of Jesus' life she connected with blood, shame, guilt, sin, hell, violence and tragic spectator sports.

"Yes," she told me in late spring as we stood on S street, in Washington D.C., books on our chests, sun on our cheeks, "there was also the glory of his dying for us. But why is that true? I feel he wanted us to know that there is no death. I'd say that's pretty good news. Oh, the glory came so late in the game that what I took away was the shame. Shame for being born a woman, for feeling my sexuality and shame for simply being imperfect and guilty as all get-out."

She stood there awhile. Were her lips quivering?

"Shame for not being born a boy, a priest, or a nun. Now why should I care what they think of me? Hell, these are people who chose not to live or feel or dance or have sex. They need therapy." She turned a long face into mine. "Deep down?" The words so soft, "I wanted their approval."

Lucy had thought long on this. Her own inner life was held up to her as somehow blasphemous in the light of Christ's purity. "I don't buy it," she said. She was already on her way to a well- thought out debauchery. This was her way of cleansing out the bad beliefs and replacing them with loving thoughts about herself. She seemed both radical and conflicted by her doubts.

I admired her irreverence. Smacked by the radical tone of her thought, I inhaled the way she rolled the four letter words, F*** Bloody Goooorgis. (Later I would love that she was speaking up for a whole passel of women who were almost ready to say "yes" to themselves.) She talked as a way of cleansing herself of simply being born female, a pantheist, and full of juice and vinegar. She described a huge split down her middle; on one side was her real self with all those sensual, excited, creative and adventurous feelings and loving thoughts.

Her other side was given her by a culture in fear of the body, of God, of the feminine, and all feelings of bliss, ecstasy and extreme emotions. This side housed a judgmental, guilty and sorry being who asked for forgiveness but always felt wrong and alone. Religion asks women to take on one 'role' and not to rock the boat.

Was it that boatload of Pilgrims who focused on sin, guilt, shame and sexuality as bad and forgot about the 'Good News?' And how all souls are equal? And it is through the heart that life is lived? Not perfect manners or squashing your feelings? Possibly.

Years late Lucy gave up the church and became an actress. I know she brought her own resisted feelings to be shared and through this catharsis allowed others to feel and question. One reason, I believe, why I love plays and film. She walked right through her fear into feeling and beingness. I lost track of her. Still, I know she would have enjoyed a sensual/ spiritual bath of sudsy awareness.

Even after the most ecstatic experience, I end up here, in the bathtub of sudsy awareness. The body, like the earth, is my anchor. What to do? It seems to be wired for pleasure and profound suffering. Try as I might I cannot stop them! All these feelings! Rage, anger, love, jealousy, guilt, joy, fear, sexuality and all shimmering up the spine and into the viscera, and, at times, seething through the yoni.

When I just stay with them, and let the feelings be free to move and radiate into all cells of my body, express the anger, sadness, grief, joy and open to all of them, I end up a wet noodle; shifts have taken place, a new spaciousness follows.

I die into the water. Do you remember St. Augustine? He asked, "to die before I die." He was a lover of life's pleasures, and yet? He knew he must love God more. "Let this little persona die to the infinite Self that I am." He wasn't afraid of pleasure, as long as he gave it all back to the Infinite One.

So what about those dark feelings? Rage, shame, jealousy, and oh, guilt? Great! Maybe they only seem dark because we keep them shut away as if they are the "me" I believe is real; all which brings up fear, which makes me feel alone. Bad. Not so. Let them roll out of the cave of the sub-conscious, the cave of the belly, where they have been stuffed. They are taking up so much room that my bones get hard, my body gets rigid, age comes from this terrible resistance to simply *feeling*. Simply *feeling* all my feelings.

Sound simple? And yet on this road I meet so many unable and so afraid of feelings. And what is more, there is no room for the Love. It takes much energy to keep down the truth of the feelings. Much energy to pretend to be someone else than what you are feeling. So what time is it? It is time to give up the good little girl and good little boy routine and become the one who feels all, embraces all, trusts all and speaks the truth in each moment. Go authentic. Truth is freedom. Truth is beauty. Truth is love. Gandhi said, "Truth is God," Yes.

*

Feelings take me beyond the little monkey mind into the deeper sensations of the body. Realization takes place in the depth of consciousness, through the body in the very cells. Take a deep breath here, right into this heart that we share with all creation.

The body is a tangle of sensations. When I touch myself just about anywhere I feel sensations; if I do it with the intention of feeling pleasurable I can really allow myself to feel high. The body is just a pool of sensations, an ocean of sensation. The skin is one seamless web of pleasurable feeling. Yes, you say, what does this have to do with the JOY of enlightenment? The ecstasy of divine union?

The manifest world and all creation came about through desire and is in a sexual dance at all times. It is by attraction, by sexuality that the entire universe and all realms were created and continue to be created.

It is how all human beings were birthed. Desire, attraction, and sexual merging. So all these sensual feelings when appreciated, when embraced, when allowed to flow bring me back to loving my Self. In reality, feeling is a bridge; "I feel my way to the Soul. " To resist anything that arises means to split myself off from the whole which is the holy. To pretend, to remain aloof from what is arising in the body/mind means to create a rift and a separation. The body, like the world, is a neutral event. If I am here to allow all that arises, I can let go of the names and see all feelings as a call to embrace. A sacred arising.

Lalla

Lalla is a favorite dancer and poet of mine. She lived in Persia in the 13th century, where, during the day, she can be found selling onions and garlics in the village. In a blink she drops her wares, leaps about, begins to shake, and ends up chanting and dancing through the streets. Her saris unravel from her body and she is dancing naked through the marketplace. She is revered by all who know her as she is filled with God's ecstatic grace.

One day she was asked, "But Lalla, why do you go naked?"

"Why not?" She answered, "I see no men around here."

Only men who were God conscious or open to the call were "real" men to her. Ponder on that one!

Lalla felt no resistances and no need to hide herself. She was drunk with love and she let that Godstream move her into flowing dance as followers answered the call. Being from India, she was able to show her devotion in deeply felt and what seems to the west, fantastic and exotic ways. Embracing herself and allowing those feelings to dance her, sky-clad and God-intoxicated.

How could you not love her? Or want to nestle in her lap as she called out, "Garlics! Two for two!" Joy and devotion and praising the Nameless One is closer to the truth of who we are than all the bickering ver dogma and belief.

My Yoga studio was in W. Concord, Massachusetts. The devotion of India was a bit too exotic for most New Englanders. Yet, the Universal Christ or the Mystic tradition was full of dance, of sensuality and of seeing all as the offspring of the loving Presence. Many came to chant with Krishna Das for hours, crammed hip to hip in the small studio. Perhaps the invitation to allow the heart to be known is rising everywhere.

So the joke is truly on us, isn't it?

The Kingdom of heaven is right here and now. Yes, you may have to 'dig' for it. a bit. May have to relinquish some old shibboleths. Let go of belief in a persona, a body-mind. Out of a belief in separation, a belief in lack and shame some made life into a hell. Always just a thought away is heaven. Where are your thoughts?

*

As I float in my bubble tub, water tickling, skin tingling I raise my cup to Jeshua, Lucy and to Lalla. Thank you all for showing me that without allowance of all that arises without embracing this body, withouts allowing the love of creation to flow through, I am lost, in lack and in conflict..

All the while the Sufi Mystics call to join them in the Divine Romance. And the mystics of the universal Christ call out Love, Love, Love, and in Heaven they all dance to the tune of the Beautiful Blue Danube. They never get into an argument about whether it is a sexual or spiritual dance. It is all that is, wrapped in a shimmering of Grace.

-EB, 2010.

I have come to admire the exotic flavor of India's devotional love for the Beloved. It is in reality a Divine Romance in which there is no separation between Creator and Created. I AM THAT I AM. There is only One dancing this dance of creation.

Goddess dancing has been spreading over the planet; the call to gaze within and to observe the persona mind is springing up all over the globe. Women are gathering and learning how to take back their power, how to leave off being victims, how to come into abundance and yet keep their hearts open.

Men are finding their heart opening to a new way of sharing their strength. Our heroes are those who build community, grow our food, bow to the Goddess, the feminine within. Now? We know we are light beings; yes, our cells give off light and at our core, we are the universal Christ, the Beloved of the Sufis, the Buddha nature and the Infinite all wrapped into the One.

We are coming to know that there is only the ONE. WE are beginning to breathe through the heart as we choose the frequency at which we want to live. We are being reborn into the realization that love, the very fire of creation, is the highest frequency of all. We are one holy baby waking up. And, even more? That Existence, life itself, is the greatest miracle of all.

SPRING AGAIN

Intimacy into -me-see
  Listening is an act of love

The greatest gift I can give to another human being is to
see them as a Soul, perfect, innocent and eternal. And to hold
space for their experience, for their feelings, for all that confusions
and their fears without intruding my thoughts. To say nothing and
simply be present is a great gift.

Ask merely; "tell me more."
It is not helpful for me to compare my experience, or to try
to make them happy. These deepest of feelings have messages;
they ask me to surrender all I thought I was. It takes me to the
edge of the persona self.
Are you able to hold space for another? Or do you try to
make them happy? Or let them know how happy you are? Does
it make you uncomfortable, hearing their sadness?

Make your home in the breath

Pondering:

Gazing into another's eyes while eating a salad is a way of making love. Try it. Enjoy and laugh as you sink deeper. Realize you are Soul-gazing. I am aware of your being aware of my being aware of you. Delight in overcoming the social anxiety that often comes with being seen and truly seeing.

Wonder Q:

Are you able to allow love to flow through you and therefore, through another?

Breathing together with the feelings is another way. There is a divine into-me-see, intimacy which allows grace to flow. Truth allows the armor of secrecy to lift. Lovers with the shared intention of celebrating sacred union find a unity unknown in most relationships based on survival or fear of being alone.

For it is not looking for God alone, it is also illuminating the Divine through conscious intention, shared breath, and true revealing of self. This shared awakening of two souls opens a gateway which must be experienced.

Q: *Where have you shut down your sacred sensual flow of feeling?* Sacred sexual union is a portal to freedom.

The silent soul gaze allows love.

It is ecstatic. It is bliss-filled.
I begin to feel a sense of freedom.
As I hold space for others I notice that
They too begin to release self-judgments.
We see clearly, not as ego, not as flawed,
Not as persona, but as a shining Soul.
With love and acceptance we gaze, Soul into Soul.
All is known.
 We sit in allowance as awareness resonates.
We speak only Truth.
Peace, acceptance and joy follow.

When we allow love to flow together there is no desire to "get" something from a partner; merely to give and receive. Not in words but in the heart awake and open. We perceive another through their bodies; even the clothes, textures, color they wear. Their skin, eyes, voices. Is the voice alive or monotone? Our bodies hold

"When two come together who, looking within, see no lack, divine grace flows." [42] The male bows to the Divine as the feminine surrenders to the Divine.   Sacred sensuality flows from and through the heart.

Tantra - Breathing together

allowing the flow of sensuality of feeling

Ask your partner to hold space for you; this is what into-me-see is truly about. Sit back to back or simply sit across from each other.

Breathe the sensual feelings up from the pelvic area, yoni/lingam (jade gate and jade sword), through the spine to the third eye. Then, breathe the energies down again. It is best to make a circle of the energies, breathing the energy up the back of the spine and then down the front of the spine. This allows the energies to radiate through the chakras and all the cells. If you are alone, allow this sensual energy, breathe it through.

I begin to remember that the body is a neutral event. And it is the temple of spiritual/sensual energy. Sacred sensuality is a choice. The one who allows the most love to flow through is the one whose life bears much fruit.

Pondering

Letting it all go

All forms vibrate at different frequencies. All creations, then, are finally impermanent. Form moves into spirit and back into form. As we now know, form is simply a bit denser kind of frequency; it is still spacious, open and skylike.

Sit and imagine all that you know leaving. That means friends, houses, cars, children, mates, thoughts, beliefs, all of it. All that makes up your world now. And then?

Yourself. The body/mind goes away.

See it all as a play. For in truth? This world is simply a moving flow of colors, shapes and shadows in an eternal field of awareness. All of it arises through the Oversoul. Through you.

Many dimensions are part of this field that we cannot see. Perhaps we are part of a three dimensional field moving into 5th, and 6th. Attune to your Essential Self and then see.

The Doorway

memoir - The Doorway

*When will you know Peace? When nothing is unacceptable to you, for
you shall have chosen to wrap all things in the allowing embrace of
Love, and you will know you are the freedom you have been seeking.*

⁴³

Florida, 1999.

During the years my father spent before entering a
nursing home I watched my mother lose her health. She tried to
care for him even as her body was ailing. She took on his bouts
of rage and confusion, his falling down, his refusal to
communicate and his refusal to call 911. She took in his sudden
angers and his deep suffering and regrets. He felt he had failed
in this world. For so long he had been the center of her life and
she loved him unconditionally. Even as he worked himself into
a bundle of misery she was at his side, bewildered.

During these months I envisioned and prayed for two
things: I asked that before he leaves his body he comes into a
state of love, a true experience in the body, a realization that is
undeniable. Secondly, I asked that after leaving this plane, he
let my mother know that he is still here so she will know the
truth of her own Soul.

I asked knowing I was heard. Praying is knowing the
truth and then, asking for it to be manifest.

A hard drinking, hard joking and hard partying man, I
saw him rarely at peace. Perhaps he could not trust the world or
even his own family. Yet, I wanted him to know that he was
loved. I added to this prayer, "If it is in his highest good and
the highest purpose of creation." For what do I know is best for
anyone? Even for myself. I felt how deeply he suffered. I
wanted for him what had changed my life - to truly feel and

255

know divine love. It took hold of my inner life; each morning I sat and asked. I sat and saw him, as I never had, at peace.

He had mastered the art of subterfuge. Hiding his feelings under his boyish jokes, still there was a happiness he reserved for his dogs, his buddies and his games. He worked so hard to get approval, to be noticed and to be "someone." He never knew that, for me and my sister Katherine, as children, he was a hero just by being our father.

If I could spread this knowing from the mountaintops and over all the fathers in the world, I would. For men, you must know this and live up to the heroic light the child sees within you and around you. To know that all you say and do is taken in by them. You are the hero of their world and your praise is a treasure and a touchstone in their lives.

The cancer left his skin sensitive. He yelled when touched. Two weeks before he finally let go, my mother and I were standing by his bed as he was sleeping. For seven years he had berated her with a torrential rage. She had cried and she had questioned, "Why this now, and why at me?"

"Who knows?" I would say, "Maybe he is not supposed to take the anger with him." Little comfort in this, her eyes said.

He woke up, green eyes sliding in lids swollen purple and thick with drugs and tears. Motioning us to roll up his bed, he grabbed our hands. A streaming flow coming from his eyes he turned to her, "I have looked for you all my life. And I found you. You are the love of my life." He turned to me to tell me how much he loved me. Between us this had happened rarely, and tears came up all around. He continued to talk about how he loved my sister Katherine, and all the family.

My mother's face broke into pure shock as she asked, "What is wrong with you?"

"Mom," I whispered, "go with it."

Afterwards he fell into a deep sleep.

When he woke up he had no memory of his epiphany and called for chocolate cake. When my father passed on my mother told me she wanted to stop eating and would I come to be with her? She said she had no reason to live now.

Her truth came with a great sadness.

"You know Mom, there is me and Katherine." I offered. "We could go on that trip to the south you always wanted."

"No." She was defiant. "Believe me in this. And I don't want the operation to fix the aneurism."

I told her I would come back in two weeks and would she eat until then? This was around Thanksgiving. Two weeks later she called one morning, excited. "You won't believe what happened. I am coming up there for Christmas; and I am going to have that operation." Elated, her voice, like a young girl's, trilled.

Finally, a week later, alone in my sister's family home, my mother pulled me into her room.

"Now, listen to me, I woke up to find your father sitting on the end of my bed."

"Was it a dream?" I questioned.

"No. He was more real than you are."

The words press into me.

"He was so handsome. He was forty five years old again. There was that look, do you remember it? How he looked at me with that same look, so boyish and full of love that he had back then." My beaming mother.

257

"What next?" I asked.

"He got up, waved me a kiss and then faded into the wall." She sat complete and at rest.

Thank you Beloved. Thank you, thank you. "Mom, what a gift!"

"I cried all night. All night," she whispered, tears upwelling. "It was more real than, than this!" Her eyes cutting to take in the room. "I have been praying that he will come back." She grabbed me with her eyes. "Will he?"

"Mom, who knows? I don't. It must take a lot of energy to do that. But, as you know now, anything is possible."

Blowing her nose, pulverizing the handkerchief, she continued. "Now listen. Don't you tell anyone, or they will think I am as crazy as you are."

Over the years I had given her books; *Autobiography of a Yogi, Ramakrishna Parables, Love without Conditions* by Paul Ferrini and the *Dialogues on Awakening* by Tom Carpenter. She had begun reading them; because now she knew something firsthand - she knew there was no death. The change in her was immediate, a calm softened her forehead and eyes. She was open now to whatever transpired.

*

The operation on her aneurism failed. The doctor kept this from us. Now came the days of pushing and pulling those limbs and that body to respond and carry her, once again, out of those cement walls, that bed, and into the light of day. Physical therapy left her in agony.

Exhausted she told me one day, finally, "No more. I am ready. Dying is just being bone-tired and wanting to go to sleep."

Breathing problems required an oxygen tube inserted in her throat. With no second thoughts she asked me to unhook her and let her go. To spend "even one minute of time" in a nursing home would not be her way. With a mind bright and without questions and a body that no longer held her vertical she chose to leave. So it was done.

But where is what I started for so along ago.
And where is it unfound?   *-Walt Whitman*

Transparent and with little flesh she looked shot through with a clear crystal light. This softness, with no hard edges and no resistance, invited silence. She became present and beamed as if newly born.

I was with her to unhook the tube and allow her to go. As I sat with her, as the morphine let her drift away, she sank into the sheets. Her body rose and fell, moved by her spirit as it gathered within. A smile came and a deep resonant sigh. I sat into the night as the flotsam of the mind and the body rose, then wrestled to be free. It felt like a meeting of her disparate parts, as though everything in her was called by a head mistress to come to attention.

Or perhaps her cells were squeezing out old tensions, old unfinished business and worries. Or, no, more than that, as if old patterns, old thoughts, were spilling off of her, rising as the sea foam of a wave. Spilling into the room that which had made up the flux and flow of her moments, memories, loves, gestures on the earth. Her unique vibration, like a Chopin melody or a fragment from the Sound of Music, was shaking off the debris and wending its way home. These visions, these dreams and visions of a young girl expecting and yearning for something from this thing called life?

Did you find it Mom? Did you?

This then was a question I so wished I had asked her. Why had I waited so long to be interested in her life? Wait Ma, wait. But she was being pulled along, perhaps by some sprite of the other world whose job was to escort her home. Now, I saw the pure fearlessness of her choice. Her leaving seemed to be giving me some old secrets, blessing me just as my grandmother had done.

And now this was my mother's last offering, this, her hidden life, this intimate cellular whirring, radiant, a confusing and rag-tag of a life, so many loose threads trailing in the breeze. Beyond thought and a loose knit array of images and feelings. An earthly affair. Now, she is freed to enter a new Godstream, a new adventure.

*

For the next two days my mother floated, carried by an invisible cloud of longing and sighs. Breaths came in spasms or sank within her. The things that she had carried with her during what she called "her" life were no longer tying her down. They flew before me: circles of yellow roses, a French cologne, the feeling sensation of a clean warm towel; humming *It's A Wonderful World* along with Louis Armstrong; the peering eye of a bay horse she had ridden once, her hands so long fingered and fine trembled and then went still.

Then there was the parade of dogs and children washed, fed, potty trained, and led along aisles of food; and houses painted and scoured, all walking into and out of that life. Yellow roses in the backyard, always the yellow roses. Nervous breakdowns with migraines and then healing. Loving to dance and yet? Sitting alone. Suffering. Only cocktails became antidotes to this loneliness.

What else: Rosa's hands rubbing her back, my mother's hands rubbing our backs, her two laughing granddaughters, the rapturous relief of the body as it falls into cool white cotton sheets, the tang of a martini on her tongue, the Indian silk coats with their gold and peach weavings.

Her handsome son-in-law, Jack, in his white uniform, on his sailboat; the cigarettes she smoked in the bathrooms so as not to upset us; sunsets and summer up to her knees in sand, those long red toenails, those feet gritty and swollen with heat, the ocean alive and bracing her against falling, and she falling back, letting it hold her.

Earthly loves. Earthly dreams. Drink. Eat. Sleep. Dress up. Again. And Love, finally, came to rule.

Now as this fades, what more? South Carolina, the place she loved most of all. Why, didn't he, my father, take her everywhere from Japan to the Panama Canal? All of those Southern women friends, with long arms burning under the orange sun, skin darkening, sucking it up, hats hovering, chatting, sponges to the sizzling heat, together, gathered on streets and porches, on the sand, faces harboring all that could not be said except in sighs and "Yes, oh, yes, we all must change and ? Why? How can it be?"

The life force gathering as the body runs down. I feel the hand that nests in mine, the clamminess gone. All the fizz fading. The heart beating, so gently. Deeper, she drops deeper, into those waters of release and of surrender, moving into silence, moving into the palm of my hand.

Where? What? The Sound of Music. Yes, I could hear
her humming it again. How she watched it over and over and
over again, because it made her so happy. I wished her a
thousand voices all singing her happiest songs. My sad bluesy
songs were not her ticket. I let the regret ride through me; that
during her last month we hadn't watched it again. My choice.

I am carried on this melody and this, the poignant
wonder, the glory and the tragedy of what it means to be in a
body. All the joy filled mornings of childhood and the
realization of this leaving, alone. Her desires and loves had
formed her just as mine have formed me.

At the end she knew that only love is real. Until we
realize this, until we realize that love is the engine of creation,
we dabble and meander, looking for love from mates and fame
and money. Yet, this ever-flowing Love is ontological, the glue
and woof of creation, the ground and shimmer of our being.

Until we know this, we will suffer.

For her, it was my father that first represented love. He
fell from that pedestal, for awhile, until he came to her after his
death. Now? She knew that we go on and he waits for her
along with her mother and father and her old friends. Those
who had seen her and loved her without conditions. Those she
had loved. Waiting for her. That was enough.

But was it?

I still questioned. Did she know, for certain, as the world
began to fray at the edges, all definition gone? Only my hand
holding hers; the mother now, I am holding the child, the child
the mother, sisters again and then the diving together as the
world body fades and her spirit is freed. Fear comes and the
breath chokes her, then the calm as the movement of that

262

burning presence in the Soul is fanned by something deeply felt but nameless, pulling her onward. On the exhale, breathtaking. Now breathless, on the exhale she lets go.

It is not for me to know, now. Not until that time when I, too, say, are you ready for me, Beloved? Mind releases, body gone. This shaky persona, too, melts away. So it is said. On into the clear light without expectation, sinking into the unknown. The Divine takes her child in the apron of her love, "Olley, olley in-come-free. Come, you are safe here. You are always safe. You have always been mine, always, playing in the field of the Lord."

-EB

It is time to realize that you are, in Reality, unlimited Light. Yes, this pure Awareness, that which you are in truth and reality.

I began to appreciate the power there is in silence.

As I truly began to drop into silence my life changed. Moving more slowly I began to appreciate it is pure intelligence. And Love.

When you are overwhelmed by the world, feeling unable to figure anything out, breathe fully and deeply. See the breath as light, feel surrounded and held by this Light. Know you are in a sea of light and love. Be still and listen. Listen deeply. You are held. You are embraced. You are the silent peace and the deep unwavering happiness in which everything arises and falls away.

In April of 2015, I travel, once again, with my friend and Casa guide Ashamarae to be with a small group at the Casa of San Dom de Ignacio de Loyola in Brasil.

This year, before the group joins together, Ashamarae and I are sit in the village of the Casa, in the back room of Fruttis, a restaurant of chia mousse and mango omelettes. Trees, flowers, butterflies and dragonflies float on the spears of sunlight. It is a tropical bubble- like sitting in a 5th or 6th dimension universe. Ashamarae is a great friend.

I tell him about a game given to us by a Zen friend Peter Ralston. Here is how it goes; David and I sit together and one says , "Experience who you are and communicate that to me." The other sits in presence and shares what (s)he notices. This may be thoughts, feelings, sensations, memories, objects, whatever arises. I ask Ashamarae the same question. He says, "I am Shiva. I am Krishna. I Am That." He looks ferocious; then he looks at me and says sharply, "You are Anandamai Ma, be her now!"

In that moment the world of Fruttis falls away.

In that blink there is a pull away and then sensations of flowing into a moving vortex of light, of light-beings and of music soft and entrancing and inside of myself. There is no "me", just this pure awareness, highly charged. Holding me is a flowing circle of light and teachers I know and love. And light surrounding all, flowing. Softness as if we are weaving spirit as one shimmering dance. Yet? Only stillness. Yogananda and

Anandamai Ma and others are here. There is a rush and then, I am gently pushed out of the circle still in an expansive state.

A darkness, a void and a strangeness follow. The fullness of me is still surrounding the body that seems there, but beneath me. No longer "mine" it simply is a body. Someone asks me questions and takes my hand and leads me down an unknown hallway and all is in shadows. I have no idea of my name, where I am, what I am doing or even that I am married. There is no fear and no worry, just curiosity,

As a channel for St. Germain, Ashamarae is guided to assemble our group of twenty people and to ask them to sit in presence and pray for me. After some time the faces take on the familiar. I share a few sentences to describe my experience, words follow. It is like crossing back into another land, another dimension. Yet? Right here where we are.

Without memories or desires I am undressed and put into bed. A friend, R., invites me to sleep in her room so she can keep me from falling; I wobble. Two days later, with their loving help, I am in the body once again.

Since then, much is being revealed. I ask. I surrender. I know now that we are held always within this Infinite loving Presence which gives us everything. The blessings of food, light, water, each arising, each event, each call to come home. Peace continues. Experience continues. Spiritual experiences, thrilling as they are, leave their perfume. They are not the main event, they are not sought. Life as it is, once you learn to see, bears witness every moment to the wonder, beauty, and ever Presence of God as our very Self. And?

As all there is.

-EB 2019

The Breaths

Do the recharge in the morning and at night. The body picks up tensions during the day. Tensions picked up over many years. Perhaps lifetimes. How does it feel? Deep relaxation takes time; it is a process.

Recharge
Your intention determines how the recharge affects you. It awakens, relaxes, refreshes and releases stress all at the same time. I do it every night and once during the day. It releases any tension I have picked up during the last day, week, year or lifetime.

This recharge is given by the Yogi/Christ Paramahansa Yogananda. In his book, *Autobiography of a Yogi,* he said this recharge was of great benefit to the over-all health of humankind. Foremost, this recharge helps to balance the oxygen and the CO_2 in the bloodstream.

Tension in the bones and muscles is also released through the deep relaxation that follows. This recharge allows the cosmic prana (life energy) to be received through the nadis- the channels of energy- which carry the cosmic life energy throughout your being. Plain english? It opens the stuck and clogged passages, both physical and etheric, which keep the flow of health alive.

Prana: Creation, awareness, holy spirit, chi, Od, light, cosmic energy, the Zero point field, vibration, Love, God. The Recharge - a mind- body tension release

Recharge

Do the recharge gently at first. Best done on the back.
but can be done in a chair, or in bed. Once you master it you
can do it standing. If you are on the floor and the back tenses,
place a pillow under the knees.

Begin with the right arm: Lift the arm 3 inches above the
floor and tense it as you inhale. Hold the breath and the tension
for the count of three, then exhale and let the arm fall to the
ground. Inhale, lift and tense the other arm, hold tension for 3
counts, then relax it, let it fall down. Inhale, Lift your leg 3
inches above the ground, tense and hold the leg for the count of
three. Then release, feel, breathe. Recharge all four limbs in this
way.

Be gentle at first. Notice the feeling sensation after you
release the tension. Relax and feel. Full recharge: Lie on your
back. Extend legs, extend arms either above your head on the
floor or to the sides of the body. Take a deep inhale and hold the
breath, as you: tense your feet, calves, thighs, buttocks, torso,
arms, fists, and lastly, stick out your tongue; make a face. Now
the entire body is tensed. Hold the tension for the count of 5
counts. On the exhale, release the tension in reverse, from the
face, hands, down through arms, torso, legs. Your feet will be the
last to relax.

Lie still. With your Inner voice say: "I choose to let go."
Let the body be heavy. Feel the tensions release. Observe how
the breath breathes you. Notice how you feel. Relax for three
breaths. Do another recharge. Do three recharges with 3 breaths
in between. Feel the deep sense of relaxation.

After a few breaths simply sit. Be alert. Do nothing.
Sensations in the body come and go. Doubts may come. As
you are aware of them? You are not them. As you are feeling
sensations you embrace them but you are not them.

Do you see?

When you are alert to the perceptions, sensations,
thoughts, images, you have already embraced and transcended
them. You are the watcher of all that arises.

When images or thoughts arise, simply allow them to
be. No need to follow them. Thoughts arise from mystery and
fall back into mystery. They are not "yours." They are not you.

Then? Let go of managing the breath.

Sit.

Allow the stillness.

Breath #1 - The Breath of Presence

Sit in a chair with the back supported and relatively straight. The feet are flat on the floor. Put a hard pillow or two books under the feet if they don't reach the floor. Begin with this : "I am here. It is now. The past is gone, the future is mind stuff; I am willing to be present, so I may explore this arising." Take a full breath and exhale thru the mouth with an "ahhh" sound, into the low belly. Do this breath three times.

Now: Sit and notice what is arising here and now. Be attentive to the sounds and the feeling-sensations of the body. The senses are alert and open. Notice thoughts, images, memories. Notice how they arise and fall away. If emotions arise, notice. Notice how relaxed and soft the body becomes. Let the nerves on the top of the head soften, the face and eyes soften.

Now: be attentive to how the breath is breathing you. Follow it, give it all of your attention. Be wholly present to breath and the feeling sensations of the body as you allow the breath to breathe you naturally. Is there resistance to this noticing and allowing it to be as it is? You are here to notice and not to judge.

Now: The feeling of being alive of existing. Feel, surrounding you, the space, the walls, floors, objects. Feel what is behind you. Listen to the sounds, no matter how slight. Let go of naming anything; let them all come and go. Now, notice where the breath moves. Put your hands on the belly. Now on the solar plexus. On the chest. Can you feel your breath in your back? Notice: 1-Images, thoughts or memories may stream up.
2-Feelings; allow them. Notice any feelings in the belly the solar plexus, the chest. 3- You may notice that you relax out of old cares. Observe, Feel, Allow.

Breath, Science, Heart

As we now know: How we breathe has a powerful effect on our physiology. Breathing with attention improves your energy levels, calms the nervous system, detoxes the body, relieves stress and tension, and strengthens the immune system. Breathe slowly and the heart follows.

Above all? Feel the breath not as simply oxygen but as the light of the creator being received by one who allows. By the one who knows there can be no separation.

Breath and Heart

1.Breathing through the heart chakra while in a state of deep gratitude reconnects us with the hearts intelligence sometimes called 'coherence'. A deep realization of self-acceptance and compassion follow.

2. Gratitude for all the blessings of this life- the light of the sun, the skies and rain that falls, all of nature - ignites the chakras. Pause for a moment, breathe the three breaths of relaxation out of the ego mind into the heart - feel gratitude for something in your life.

3. In your nightly journal feel into your gratitude. Say 'yes' to all that arises during your day. Write down a few things you are grateful for. It can be as simple as appreciating the person who held the door open for you. The crow who called out as you passed. The blue skies.

See life through the perspective of gratitude. Laughter stops the egoic mind. I had to learn how to truly laugh. And to remember the Cosmic Joke at least once a day...

Life is movement and movement is life.

This is a breath of opening, allowing and receiving. A breath in which the cosmic prana/spirit is stabilized in all cells. "Prana" is the Sanskrit term for the cosmic light/life force/ intelligence that is everywhere at once; Spirit, Awareness, the Divine. Literally, "The playing field of the Lord." *(Lord in Aramaic: Shimmering Presence of Loving Oneness.")*

It is the very essence of all life, both visible and invisible. It is the body of the shimmering One.
In the west we call it Spirit, God, Goddess, Source, Divine Mother, Hashem (nameless one) Prana: Many english words are needed to point to the mystery of this cosmos.
I call it Holy (whole) Spirit for it is the Essence of the Infinite One. We live in this awareness Universe - magical, ever flowing, vibrant...

*It is the "flow" of this prana/chi/Holy Spirit/ pure awareness throughout your being that keeps you healthy, alert and alive.

Make your home in the breath

Breath #2 - The Heartbeat Rhythm

By joining the rhythms of the breath with that of the heartbeat you augment health, vitality and gratitude.

Sit in a chair with the back relatively straight, the arms relaxed. Feel your heartbeat or feel your pulse. Use the first two fingers of one hand, not the thumb, on the inner wrist of the other hand. Find your heartbeat and listen to it for a minute or so. Inhale through the nose for 4 heartbeats, and exhale through the nose for 4-6 beats. As you continue you may notice that the exhale lengthens, naturally.

As you continue, relaxed and breathing with the heartbeats, see if it feels good to inhale from the belly on 4 heartbeats, hold for 4 heartbeats (counts) and exhale on 8 heartbeats.

The breath should be comfortable and steady. The rhythm is unique for each person. Do not rush it.

It will feel effortless if you are following the best rhythm for you. Let your attention come into the breath, the heartbeat and the feeling-sensations of the body.

No hurry. Notice if thoughts and images stream through. Notice. Let them unfold. Let them arise, notice, then bring your awareness to the breath. Witnessing, allowing, relaxing into this moment.

Then, come into the breath of Presence #1. Relax into the stillness. It is here, in this doing nothing, simply being with what is arising that the fruit of the breath is known. Do nothing. Simply "be." The Viloma breath and prana

Students, when asked to give one word to express the feeling sensation of this Viloma breath have replied, "grounded." Or "spacious."

Q: What is your feeling word? Sit after completing the breath. Sit and observe how the breath breathes you. Then, find the stillness. Be aware of this awareness.

Viloma breath

Feel the breath as pure light, golden or white. With each inhale, do not take little breaths but feel as though your body is this spacious field and is entirely filled with the pure wave of breath. Feel the breath and the awareness as a cloud which enfolds you beyond the membrane of skin and throughout the room, town, cosmos. You are always one with Source.

Allow.

Come to the Viloma Breath at least once a day for a month. Then, add the Lovesbreath each morning. Lovesbreath is the best breath for truly feeling into the low belly, softening a frozen diaphragm and exploring the body. And the body's resistances.

It is given to us to for the allowing of hidden feelings, old wounds and fears to arise. As a child they were too scary. Now? You know you are supported. You have friends. You are also held in this field of pure knowing.

Breath #3 - The Viloma Breath

A Retention Breath

This is a complete yoga inhalation carried out in five stages. During this breath the diaphragm opens while the lungs expand. The internal organs and the brain are stimulated while control of the abdominal muscles is enhanced. All of this happens during the slight retention of the breath.

Let the breath fill from the feet, legs, and belly upward; as if you are filling a glass with water. This Breath may be followed while walking, lying down, in a yoga asana, or sitting in a low chair. I suggest a chair with feet flat on the floor or on a dense pillow if your feet don't reach the floor. Before beginning, take your pulse. The heartbeat will become a metronome. As you follow its beat you bring harmony to your entire being.

Begin: Inhale through the nose, hold one count. Inhale again, hold one count. Inhale three more times, and on the third inhale, hold your breath again for a 3 count - what feels comfortable. Then slowly exhale through the mouth. Let the exhale continue until the body is soft and relaxed. Feel the moment between inhale and exhale. The stillness. Then start the cycle again.

A series of five complete inhalations, a short retention, followed by a continuous exhalation forms one cycle of the Viloma breath. Do a series of five cycles and then rest. Close the eyes. Now bring all your attention to how the breath breathes you. Sit and be attentive now to the sounds around you. All sensations, feelings and perceptions that are arising. Sit in the Now which is eternity.

Sit in Presence. Allow it, be with it. What do you feel?

Saying a name of God whether it is Lord, Ram, Amma or Shiva in Hinduism, is called "Japa nama." Japa purifies the mind and brings the attention into the heart. It is said that the first mantra given to humanity was "Om Nama Shivaya." It comes in many melodies and brings a softness to the heart and mind. Sometimes it begins to sing itself to me. Instead of the whacky persona mind, I hear a mantra. Then I sing and invite others to sing. Chanting raises the frequency all over the planet.

"Japa helps to purify the mind so love can be mind's controlling impulse."
                                                                Shri Babaji

The sound of God's name IS God. Do you see? This is Vedic wisdom. It is said that the sound *Yahweh* in Hebrew is a breathing sound rather than a word. I have found Japa steadies the energy while I am at the grocery store or waiting in a line.

Instead of worry, feel Japa in the heart spreading into all the cells of your being. MA AUM (divine love, divine light) is a japa that Amma, the hugging Saint, teaches her friends.

Breath #4 - The Ujayyi Breath

Often called "the oceanic breath" or "the upward victorious breath," this is the foundation breath of Yoga; the only one used during asana practice, walking, doing the dishes. It tends to heighten every experience by bringing attention instantly within.

Sit in a relaxed position either in a chair with feet flat on the floor, or in a seated yoga position. Sit with the back relatively straight. Now pretend you are blowing on and cleaning your glasses; the way you blow from the roof of the mouth so that your breath is a bit moist. It is this place on the upper palate to which you must bring your attention.

You will be inhaling to a point on the upper palate near the hard palate as it turns into the soft palate. You will exhale from that same point.

The breath makes a whispering or a hushing sound. Practice inhaling and exhaling with ahhhhh and eeee sounds. On the inhale make and feel the ahhhh sound at that point on the palate. On the exhale the "eeeeee" sound. Use a bit of olive oil or coconut oil on the tongue or on the back of the mouth as this breath can make the throat feel dry when you first use it.

You know you're doing it correctly when you feel muscles in the lower belly slightly pumping; this calls on the Vegas nerve.

After breathing through the mouth with this breath, once it feels comfortable, breathe through the nose using the same technique of drawing breath to this point on the upper palate. The sound is internal, and the feeling is of pulling the breath from deep in the belly, through the spine, up to the third eye.

Then close your eyes and follow the sound and the feeling. In India many say the inner mental sound (unvoiced) of Vaaa on the inhale and Sheeeee on the exhale as the breath goes down the spine. (Shiiiiii Vaaaaaa!)

Concentration

In the older Yoga books, it is written that the Yogis run over a hundred miles without rest. They do this while breathing a certain breath which allows great endurance. It is now accepted that it is this Ujjayi breath that allows runners to go great distances without tiring. This breath is now being taught to competitive athletes.

Bill Rodgers, the well-known marathon runner, taught his competitive runners this breath. What did they find? That throughout the marathon the pulse and heart rate stays the same, both steady and rhythmic, even over great distances. Along with that, the sound of the breath within the mouth and throat draws the attention within so that focus is steady and immoveable.

Ujjayi pranayama

1) Improves concentration in any physical practice. Becoming absorbed in Ujjayi allows you to run for great distances without raising the heart rate. It lets you stay in Yoga poses for longer periods of time. It allows the attention to be absorbed within.

2. The sound brings the attention within. By quieting the mind there is a tranquility and a radiance. The waves of the brain mirror the waves of the breath.

3. All breaths help you to remain grounded in the body whether it is a still or a moving asana practice.

4. The Ujjayi breath regulates heating of the body. The friction of the air passing through the lungs and throat generates internal body heat. It is similar to a massage for the internal organs; as the core becomes warm from the inside, the body becomes prepared for asana practice.

5. Additional benefits include diminished pain from headaches, relief of sinus pressure, decrease in phlegm, and strengthening of the nervous and digestive systems.

6. Ujjayi tells us when we need to surrender into a resting posture; the breath should remain as even and smooth in the postures as when we rest.

7. In our daily life, it returns us to calm in the face of challenges. When listened to, your breath is guiding you to simply be still. The ancient yogis realized the intimate relationship between breath, calm and actions that come from the heart place rather than from the reactive persona mind.

The yogic tradition calls this type of breathing from the belly, Uddiyana, which means the throne of God or Upward victorious breath.

The Ujjayi/Uddiyana breath is the prologue to the Kriya Breath. Originally given by Shri Babaji, the deathless saint, to Lahiri Mahasaya, to Sri Yukteswarji, to Yogananda, and then to the world.

It is a powerful breath which is learned from a master of this breath. Yogananda's Self-realization Center and the Babaji centers teach this Kriya Breath.

I teach it only to one who asks and who has done other pranayam/ breathing ways.

Pondering:

Ask the wonder question: Who is it that notices my experiences? Who notices this sadness, this feeling of unworthiness? Sit with this. Feelings come and go, like thoughts. What notices and is aware of them - does it come and go?

Who or what is it that knows, that is aware of my feelings? Continue to ask this question.

Relax after a breathing. Relax the mind. "No thoughts. No words."

The power of rhythmic breathing.

The power of losing control

The waves of the brain are tied to the waves of the breath.

The connection between the breath and the mind - this you must experience yourself! It is important to simply practice the breath without thinking about what it may or may not do. It will guide you in a unique way. Do you see? The breath becomes the teacher when you begin to follow it's guidance. Now sit up and notice as you relax into Presence.

Close the eyes.

Relax deeply.

As you sit, allow all to be 'as it is.'

Allowing all to be 'as it is' means you relinquish all need to control, all need to 'make something happen.' You are here to explore where you are. What you are arises out of this deep listening within.

Sitting in Presence is never about learning or mastering a technique.

It is simply letting go of all control.

This needing control is a huge program for most souls. The message has been take control of your life. Now? I allow life to move through me. The breath teaches surrender. Surrender to the Infinite life which moves through all.

It is relaxing into what is arising where you are.

Now.

Breath #5 - The Taoist breath

This breath ignites the respiratory system. It is from Dharma's Nerve Altering Technique exercises. This is the only breath out of the twelve forms given. All twelve are for renewing the nervous system. Stand in the truth: "I am one with the Infinite One. There is no separation." Feel into the oneness; feel the breath moving through the body, the floor, the house, the surrounding earth and trees. Take three breaths to prepare.

Stand with your feet under your hips, knees soft. Put your hands in front of your face with palms facing outward. Let the right eye see the right hand and the left eye see the left hand.

As you inhale let the hands push away from the face, as if pushing a weight. Let it be somewhat slow.

On the exhale make fists with the hands and forcefully pull the arms back and down so the fists end up by your side, palm up. The exhale will be a sudden forceful one, blown out from the mouth.

Continue this seven times. Notice how the belly pulls inward with the exhale.

Then: Stand with the arms hanging at the sides. Relax while feeling the currents of movement flow through you. Let your attention move through the body entirely. Be attentive as to how the breath breathes you.

You may choose to do this breath along with the other techniques once a week. I find that it awakens the respiratory system in a gentle but powerful way. It also renews the nervous system.

Let go of expectations; yet be expectant.

Thousands upon thousands of messengers have come from all cultures to say this: The Kingdom of God is within.

You are not what you think you are. As an offshoot of the One you unfolded out of this Sea of consciousness and then? Forgot where you came from.

You are a Light that encompasses all.

The immensity is beyond the little mind.

It is all pretty simple!

And yet?

The ego uses its reason and misses truth. And walks right past Reality.

As the persona-mind collapses, the Divine shines through.

Along with me? Be surprised.

You can afford to be fearless, for when you are willing to be fearless no matter what happens, and you do not attend to the voice of separated ego, a most wonderful miracle happens.

You find that you are the power of life which transforms everything that you experience.

You know that you are the creative power that brings forth all manifest form, including the body, and that nothing can touch your holy body or the physical body unless you give it permission.[44]

Love assumes many forms; sometimes it is peace sometimes it is happiness, sometimes bliss or joy. Restlessness or sorrow. Love is the root and like a tree it has many branches spreading around.[45]

Love's Breath

The days of the prophets have never ended. The Infinite One does, indeed, continue to move through all and speak through all who ask and are willing to dive deeper and to listen.

The days of those who choose transparency and allow the light of the Infinite, the voice of love, to speak through them, has never ended.

After *A Course in Miracles* was given through the scribe Dr. Helen Schucman, there came *The Way of Mastery*. At the heart of this wisdom is Love's Breath. Forgiveness is its blood and gratitude is it's wellspring.

This was given through my mystic brother and great friend Jon Marc Hammer, or Jayem as he is known today.

In a nutshell: The year is 1988. Jon Marc is surprised during a meditation by light filling the room and a majestic light-being who asks him, "Who do you believe I am?" Being a Buddhist meditator, he replies, "Buddha?"

"I am Jeshua Ben Joseph. You have been running from me for many lifetimes."

He hears the voice and feels only this immense love and yet? His reaction is to be highly skeptical. For nine years he asks for proofs; after many, he realizes the truth. He is asked to fulfill his purpose in this life through bringing a heart wisdom to the world.

Jeshua Ben Joseph or Jesus as he is known to the west, was able to use Marc's body, voice and mind to bring, "a correction to the misinterpretations of my teachings when I was embodied."

Yes, may sound fantastic to some, but Ascended masters are the silent and unseen partners in our universe. There are many prophets, scribes, and vessels today allowing ascended masters to speak through them.

People from all over the world gathered to share this Way of Mastery, this way of peace, of no beliefs but of seeing the soul in everyone you meet. Wherever we gathered, on pilgrimages throughout Israel, California, South France, Turkey, Bali, and Italy there were ecstatic times and deeply quiet times. For hours we melded into one hilarious pool of no-mind.

We danced and danced. The barriers to trusting and the social anxiety in relationship with others comes up to be embraced. I see myself in my brothers and sisters. You can choose in each moment to remember Reality. A deep sense of contentment follows.

The Way of Mastery is given by a master teacher, Jeshua Ben Joseph and friends. Welcome to Reality. The depth and eloquence of this wisdom, the wit, humor and lightness is extraordinary. *Jeshua's teaching is the continuation of a Divine Plan which began as we, as souls, as Christed spirits, fell into time. Old wounds between tribes, as we see in the Middle East, shift and become the ground of healing.*

*

The Way of Mastery
> *Breath is the doorway to God.*
> *"Once you ask, the end is perfectly certain."*
> *All true paths of Self-realization are a direct experience of* God. *That is what this Way of Mastery is about.*[46]

Certain teachers who have come into the world have lived lives which seemed to be miraculous. They have done things that seemed to be miracles according to the collective consciousness, because they were living in that stream of knowing divine consciousness, knowing themselves to be unlimited.[47]

The Breath of Infinite love
Set your life on fire. Seek those who fan your flames.[48]

Lovesbreath
I do this breath each morning, lying on the floor on my back. Slowly feeling into this breath, a spaciousness follows. The waves of the breath begin to soften the belly and torso. Most people live with a rigid belly without being aware of tension.

As you become fully embodied (incarnated), begin to feel and sense the breath expanding and joining with the light around the body, in the room, throughout.

Through this breath much that lay hidden in the sub-conscious comes up to be seen, allowed and expressed. A great peace emerges as if something has been shaken free. Some old wound or self-hate. Some old way or belief that is false. Transformation takes hold. If you are willing.

Being willing is a great gift you must claim for yourself. With each breath let there be a willingness to surrender.

The Way of Mastery is fully and completely about transformation; at the deepest levels of the consciousness, at the cellular level. Transformation of my 'seeing' anew. Transformation from feeling a victim of the world, to mastery.

"If you would know the Love of God you must be the love of God."

When you choose to allow only love, knowledge is a mystical experience. True knowing is immediate. One who knows the Self, is the Presence of love in form.Love is in every cell of our being as the light of the Infinite.

The great Yogi/Christs of India and the East see everything as the Infinite, see all that is as this shimmering Presence. Pure

290

awareness is pure Love. It is not about ideas or words which appeal to the intellect alone.

This way dovetailed with the wisdom of Yoga, of Yogananda and India's well-known Yoga/Christs - Babaji, Lahiri Mahashaya, Krishna, Sri Yuktesvar, Ramana Maharshi, Anandamai Ma, and so many other masters.

When I encountered the book T*he Jeshua Letters*, my body trembled. I felt called back into a family. The wisdom and profound truths which came through this reluctant, and at times skeptical, scribe, Jon Marc (Jayem) "quivered my bones," as my Uncle Hank used to say. Jeshua talks of the freedom that awakening from the dream of separation brings to all.

The Way of Mastery came soon after, and I was called to step into my deepest fears. The fear of abandonment, of losing my mind, of failure, of not being worthy, of being unloveable, and the fear of death. Living as the body is all about fear, suffering and pain.

The ego is but that conglomeration..... of thoughts that make up the perception of limitation, the perception of life and death, the perception of a separate self. The ego is complete and utter fear. The body is really a manifestation of that one belief, "I am separate."[49]

Make your home in the Breath

Lovesbreath and feelings

As a child, physical and emotional pain is first felt in the heart. The heart feels as if it is closed down; this is just an idea and yet? The mind is powerful. The child closes down and feels distrust and fear. This can lead to a fear of "feeling my own feelings and expressing my real feelings." Repression of feelings leads to great misery both in the child, in the family and in the world. It is a root cause for our suffering. For in reality, my feelings are the truth of who I am in each moment.

Held in the molecules of the body, wounds are thorns. Yes, that is right and it is why the body often feels like a minefield. Many people leave the body and escape into the mind; some actually live out of body or above the neck, cut off from their sentient, feeling body. Life is lived through the filter of the persona mind. Then, the pain is pushed down into the belly. This area is then off-limits. We then may breathe in our chest or forget to breathe; the flow of life-force is shut down.

As we begin to breathe into our Dan Tien, our lower belly, transformation begins. As the breath/light pushes through the cells and molecules, these energies move and are released.

This breath is done while lying down on the back. The knees are bent with the feet planted on the floor. Separate the feet so the knees can relax against each other. For greater relaxation, place a pillow under the knees, yet keep the feet flat on the floor. Bring the hands to rest on the belly, over and below the belly button.

Begin: inhale through the nose and exhale through the nose. Let it feel like slow motion no hurry. Let the head be heavy. Let the shoulders release; the jaw release; the tongue soften.

Continue to inhale through the nose and exhale through the nose, allowing the belly button to gently relax towards the earth. Notice any resistance in the belly, in the solar plexus, in the heart area or the throat. Places that resist the breath.

As you inhale, direct the breath into the low belly; the area that includes the belly button and below. Feel it expand the belly upward, like a balloon. Exhale through the nose, let the belly button drop down towards the earth.

Take ten breaths, one breath includes both inhale and exhale. Be aware, feel if there is resistance in the low belly to expand. Be gentle. It may have taken years to create a rigid belly. See if you can direct it deep so it pushes gently against the pelvic bones. The low belly will expand and open. Continue and just feel how it feels. The muscles may feel tight at first; with practice the belly softens and opens.

Continue, Inhale and exhale, and feel. Allow the awareness to fill the belly along with the breath and the light.

The body is transfigured to allow the infinite essence of being which is always and everywhere at once, to flow, to open the heart and to bring it's wisdom to guide me in all things.

All that we desire - freedom, truth, love, creation and fulfillment is revealed as our own true nature. Is not this why we are here?

*

Loves breath brings this cosmic life force or pure spirit, into every atom, cell and molecule of the body while suffusing you with a deep sense of being held. Part #1 opens, softens, ignites through the belly where there are fears, wounds, feelings of lack and resentments.

Allowing these energies to be felt and freed brings a palpable spaciousness. The prologue is the experience. Yet? Awakening is before all experience. And beyond all words.

Loves breath #2 opens up the entire area of heart, chest solar plexus, legs, feet, arms, hands, throat and head. The breath breathes your entire being. Then the release into expansion and spaciousness, and a willingness to allow all feelings follows.
Revelation may follow.

"When the doors of perception are cleansed, everything will appear to man as it really is, Infinite."[50]

Pondering: wonder questions

Wonder questions:

Can you find a world outside your perception?

This is a question put by many yogis, rishis and old school philosophers.

Have you ever found a barrier or edge to your consciousness?

The Yogis and sages go within to discover the answers to these questions. Philosophy, at one time, asked these questions. In my reading travels I found a man, Paul Brunton, both a philosopher and a Rishi who left a canoe of books. Perfect for the intellectual and the scientist of reality.

And questions! One of these questions is about the world: *What is it made of?*

The Yogis answer? Find out for yourself. Consciousness. We know what we call the world only through our perceptions. Out of the field of pure awareness each of us creates a world. It has the appearance of Reality. (Remember? Our senses bring us around 4% of reality? Reality is within.) Yes, it collapsed my little mind.

Reality is not a collection of finite objects known by a finite self, but as it truly is, Infinite. Experience is not divided by an inside self and an outside world. There is no division. One skylike spaciousness is our womb and ocean and playground. Paul Brunton

The sage, the yogi or mystic goes Inwards. The scientist/materialist goes outward. As they each go farther and father, they arrive at the same conclusion.[51]

*Enlightenment absorbs this universe of qualities.
when that merging occurs, there is nothing
but God. This is the only doctrine.
there Is no word for it, no mind
to understand it with, no categories
of transcendence or non-transcendence,
no vow of silence, no mystical attitude.
there is no Shiva and no Shakti
in enlightenment, and if there is something
that remains, that whatever-it-is is the only teaching.

Before all experience there is consciousness.

What we call 'matter' is simply a modulation of consciousness.
Which means that we only know the world as perception. We can
never know the world apart from perception. Which, for me and
now so many others, means, there is one consciousness flowing
through all.
Each of us projects a slightly different world.
Sit. Relax. Allow the inner smile.

Lovesbreath - part II

A continuation of Lovesbreath I. A flowing breath as a wave flows on a river.

Continue to inhale through the nose and exhale through the nose. Notice any resistance in the belly, the throat, in the solar plexus, in the heart area.

Now: bring the left hand to the heart chakra, the spot right under the sternum. Place the right hand over and below the belly button. Breathe first into the low belly and then continue the inhale so the breath fills the ribs, the back, the chest, and the entire torso. Let your awareness be brought fully to the breath. Exhale. Allow it to be a complete exhale.

Now, as you inhale, direct the breath first into the low belly; then, continuing to inhale, fill the solar plexus, the stomach, the chest, the back, the entire torso. If it is easier, inhale four breaths in succession until it becomes effortless. Then exhale through the nose and feel the release and "letting go." Exhale and let the bellybutton fall towards the earth.

Take ten breaths, one breath includes both inhale and exhale. Be aware, feel if there is any resistance in the low belly to expanding. Be gentle; give it time. This breath bring softness, relaxation and a sense of release throughout your entire being.

Visualize the breath as pure light. Feel it as breath/light. All your attention is with the feeling and flow of breath.

Notice. Sense. Feel.

There is only God. There cannot be a separate me; that is an idea of the mind. What can we create this day that offers to the world the good, the holy and the beautiful? [52]

Breath

"To seek is well and good, my friend. But only in the end of seeking (which is but the recognition that God, the Power within all existence, has already found You) will you discover the truth and power of your very breath. For it is the presence of the Holy Spirit, the bridge to the mind of the Father-Mother.

You cannot step upon it and cross from illusion to Reality without fully recognizing and accepting that it is given you freely, and is already beneath your feet. Let not your practice begin until you acknowledge that the Holy Spirit is with you now and that no barriers exist separating you, therefore, from the Father-Mothers Presence."

- *Way of Mastery*

The secret of the belly

In the east there is a wisdom of the belly. In China it is called the Dan Tien, the treasure field. Here (about 2 inches below the navel), it was found, if one cultivates Dan Tien, the life force gains in vigor and stability. Many spiritual traditions point to the low belly as a sacred area and many say, "this is where you meet the mountain and this is where you meet God within."

*

In the Japanese tradition it is called, "Hara."

Lovesbreath directs you to the sacred area of the Dan Tien or hara. Moving energy from here creates space. Collecting energy here, allowing the awareness to drop into this place, the mountain, the ocean of light, may bring a great peace, a great meeting, a great union.

The seat of true intimacy (into-me-see), this sacred place defines what union is. This spirit of life which fills the body is called at times Ki, chi, prana, light or Holy Spirit. Play with this breath, enjoy it, delight in it, do not try to get any place; no expectations. Just feel, sense, and bring your attention here.

Then sit and listen and drop deeper within.

In truth, the world is of your making. As I learned to accept the ego's falsity, as I learned to 'see', the world became innocent. A safe place as long as you are in Presence, as long as I remember who I AM in truth. We are moving now into a most beautiful place of knowing that we are in the world but not of the world. We are moving into the space of being okay with that. That is a great leap in perception.

When you struggle and you wonder what it is all about, ask for help. Know that the universe is listening. Then remember the power in the breath and breathe. And as you take that deep breath, what do you feel? Calm. You feel the comfort that comes with that deep breath, the peace. [53]

Reader: I truly dislike lists. So read on by if you wish. In my defense, there are but three lists in this book.

These teachings help to correct the mind, heal the heart, and awaken the soul. Breath is the bridge to the Soul-The Christed spirit. Here in a nutshell. All beings are a spark of light. We are each fully responsible for how we use the Light to choose and thus attract precisely what we experience. As a sovereign soul this power of choice is the most fundamental aspect of our reality.

- God is Love, and Love does not condemn; there is no judgment. Love without conditions accepts all things, allows all things, embraces all things, trusts all things. And thereby transcends the world.
- All beings are to be forgiven and supported (if they are willing) to transform their orientation from fear to Love.
- Only when we forgive, and then find ways to serve this 'At-one-ment' may we truly awaken to a full enlightenment and enter Mastery.
- Forgiveness is a radical transformation of one's being, best encapsulated in the Aramaic term, washwoklan: to return to Original Wholeness.
- While our Union and Reality is unchanged, unchanging, and unchangeable, we have chosen to imagine and create the experiences that flow from a belief that we have achieved Primal Separation. We each create the world we see. Know this now.
- This is the true meaning of 'hell'. Though often hidden, separation engenders a Primal Guilt, the 'dysfunctional' sense of our inner being that gives birth to the myriad forms of psychological and behavioral sufferings of humanity.
- Heaven, like hell, is available to all beings willing to enter and go through the purification, healing, and waking process of enlightenment. Heaven is as equally 'here' as in any of the infinite realms of Light beyond this world.
- Sin is not a moral failing but a being off the path of Self-realization, a resistance to knowing and living this Light.

301

Lovesbreath and feelings

As a child, physical and emotional pain is first felt in the heart. The heart feels as if it is closed down; this is just an idea and yet? The mind is powerful. The child closes down and feels distrust and fear. This can lead to a fear of "feeling my own feelings and expressing my real feelings." Repression of feelings leads to great misery both in the child, in the family and in the world. It is a root cause for our suffering. For in reality, my feelings are the truth of who I am in each moment.

Held in the molecules of the body, wounds are thorns. Yes, that is right and it is why the body often feels like a minefield. Many people leave the body and escape into the mind; some actually live out of body or above the neck, cut off from their sentient, feeling body. Life is lived through the filter of the persona mind. Then, the pain is pushed down into the belly. This area is then off-limits. We then may breathe in our chest or forget to breathe; the flow of life-force is shut down.

As we begin to breathe into our Dan Tien, our lower belly, transformation begins. As the breath/light pushes through the cells and molecules, these energies move and are released.

Grace

The long and short path

The questions come up; what am I holding onto? What am I holding against? Where am I sure I am right? Only the ego believes it is right. The breath penetrates all emotional attachments. The fear of life, of allowing love to flow through me fully, is a central program for many on the planet today. Into-me-see and living in complete honesty with my partners and friends becomes a touchstone.

As I breathed, felt and sat and went about my life remembering the spaciousness of my being, my Christed nature, shifts begin to take place.

The observation of how the ego reacts, the deeper programs was once called the Long Path. Some forgot that there is Grace; you don't have to get so entangled with your shortcomings that you forget the BIG picture! The breathing of the lightbreath and the ongoing remembrance of oneness, this in itself may bring you into remembrance. Be with the spaciousness you are as one with the Absolute; this is called the short path. In the Way of Mastery both conjoin to bring all into mastery of life, of death of transparency.

The Qigong breath brings you into balance with all that is arising: the earth, the sun, the moon, the four directions and the cosmos. Moving around and within you are the currents of life called 'prana', (Yoga) which is consciousness itself. The mystery, which is life, is always arising, anew and fresh in each moment.

Do this breath slowly and with a feeling of blessing the earth with your awareness and with your breath. The frequency of the earth is the same frequency as your own body. Every organ of the body holds it's own frequency. As we breathe, relax, allow and come into Presence we harmonize our entire being with the cosmos. Presence is the portal to eternity. Now. Here.

Standing Breath between earth and heaven.

Stand on the earth if possible. Stand barefoot or with shoes that conduct the energy (wear hide/leather and not rubber or plastic which insulates rather than conducts) .

Stand with the feeling sensation of a being between heaven and earth, embracing both. Feet under the hips and planted. Knees soft. The arms open slightly behind you with the thumbs rotated backwards.

See, feel and sense the center of the earth as a diamond light below you. Above you is the sun. INHALE as you bring arms up; you bring this light through the earth and the body, into the heart and finally above the head. Feel that you are taking in all the lightbreath and prana, letting it rise. EXHALE as you slowly bring arms down bringing the light from the sun through space, through the body and into the earth.

The breath is cosmic light, prana, energy and consciousness. Feel this breath light as a stream which both enfolds you and streams through you and then into the earth. Feel the lightbreath as filled with luminous gold and white light. Feel it as a matrix field holding you.

Continue the breath at least seven times. Then rest in standing pose. This is the Mountain Asana (way of being). Let the arms hang heavy at your sides. Allow the legs to feel soft, as if they are giving into gravity. Feel the belly and the genitals relax. Notice if there is tension there. In the perineum. Let it soften. Feel deeper within, the currents of light energy/prana moving through the body.

Kapalabhati breath means "shining skull"

When first introduced to this breath in the 1970's, I found it exhilarating. On wakening in the morning with the realization I exist and am awake, I say, "I am fully embodied. I am anchored to this earth and one with Infinite Spirit." My routine is to do some slow and gentle movements with breath. Then I sit and do the kapalabhati breath.

I sit for 8-10 minutes with this breath, then sit quietly and observe; feeling the night's fogginess subside as the prana/energy begins to flow. The tingle of energy and warmth ease me into the morning, into Presence. At the end of the three rounds, in deep relaxation, I notice all that is arising; sounds, the feeling-sensations, heart beats and how the breath is breathing me. I let my attention take me deeper and deeper. Expanded, aware of this awareness, eternity is here.

While many friends were taking drugs to dive out of old habits and for recreation, these breaths allowed me to come into experiences of heightened awareness, spaciousness and a sense of well-being. For me? This breath "cleans out the cobwebs."

This Kapalabhati breath is a tonic for your whole being. Fast breathing followed by a period of calm cleanses the nadis- the channels which carry the cosmic life energy throughout your being. Go slowly.

Breath #8 - The Kapalabhati Breath.

This Breath cleans the nadis, the channels which carry the cosmic energy, throughout your being. It irrigates the brain, stimulates the belly and digestive system, and tones the organs of digestion and elimination. Go slowly. The young bird does not fly immediately but spends time strengthening it's wings.

First, put your finger in front of your face. See it as a candle that you are going to blow out. Blow the breath with power out of the mouth at the finger. Notice what happens in the body. You may feel your lower abdomen muscle pull inward as you exhale with vigor.

Generally, the breath fills up again, after the exhale, without your awareness; if not inhale through the nose.

Continue blowing softly and slowly until it feels comfortable. Notice: It is the strong pulling in of the belly muscles that thrust the breath out. Now, exhale out through the nose rather than the mouth. Feel how that feels. If there is discomfort, discontinue.

Breathing, like all of life, is a process. Give it time to become comfortable and steady. Be gentle with yourself. If the muscles of respiration have curled up and shut down, it takes awhile to let them soften, become elastic and alive.

After the first round of 15 breaths, take a relaxed 2 breaths. Then, take a slow deep inhale and let the breath/light fill up the entire torso and body. Hold for 4 counts. Then relax. Sit, as the body softens, eyes closed, feeling all that arises.

Three rounds. Begin with 15 breaths. Work up to 50 breaths a round. Sit, with eyes closed, inner gaze. Observe: how the breath breathes you.

Do not do this breath when you are ill,

307

Kapalabhati and the brain

We have much to learn from these Yogic breaths. [54]

The brain behaves like a spongy mass, shrinking and enlarging according to the respiratory rhythm. This double movement influences the circulation of fluids in the brain, especially the blood. Because the brain is the greatest consumer of blood in the body, we realize how important is the circulation in this area.[55]

The Yogic breaths, particularly kapalabhati and other bhastrika breaths, enhance the circulation of the blood. Most physiologists and yogis know that respiration, especially that done with awareness, alters the volume of the brain. Normally most people breathe at around 18 exhalations per minute. Kapalabhati is a bastrika breath, sometimes called the "breath of fire." This breath with its 120 exhalations per minute seems to actually enhance the brain.

It helps to open the capillaries in a way that wash and vitalize the brain. The endocrine glands, enfolded in the brain, the pineal and pituitary, are also enhanced through the pulsing of the breath.

Students often ask the question; is it dangerous to breathe so quickly, can pressure build up in the head? This breath has been done for literally thousands of years. Research has found that the pressure always stays at normal physiological limits within the brain; there is no danger. Only the circulation is accelerated. The results are inexpressible and felt deeply. And? You must experience it for yourself.

Sit in a room you have made into a sacred space. Begin with fifteen (15) fast breaths for all three cycles. Everyday for two weeks. Then add one more count each week. If you feel balanced and peaceful at the end of the three cycles, you are listening to the wisdom of the breath.

This Bhastrika breath is a traditional Yoga breath. It increases Prana or life force and is, therefore, very good in the morning and in the afternoon. It aides digestion by bringing energy to digestive organs. More enlivening than caffeine, I find that it helps to clear the persona minds incessant chattering.

Go slowly. The breath cannot serve you if you rush it or try to go quickly; the nervous system needs time to readjust, expand and open to this "fire" breath. Hurrying this process can lead to feeling out of balance. It can even be dangerous; this is how powerful the breath is. Cultivate a sense of attention, patience and of being methodical.

Observe sensations. Heart, solar plexus, belly, throat. Each week add around 3-5 more breaths; notice how you feel. Sit and let your attention be pulled deeper and deeper within.

Make your home in the breath

Coming into Presence

God's grace blows as the wind.
We are only asked to open our sails.   -Ramakrishna

Sit after the breath. Close the eyes. Follow the feeling-sensations of the body. Find the stillness of the body and allow the attention to drop into the heart and belly. The senses are open and alert. The breath moves on its own. All happens on it's own, without your action. Know this. There is nothing to change or fix or manage.

Feel the spaciousness surrounding the body, permeating the body and the room. One skylike space. Feel even the walls to be spacious. Feel the spaciousness that has no without or within. No expectations here. No next or after. Notice the body soften. Be with whatever is arising. No resistance. There is no waiting for anything, for you are here. Before all experience the realization of I AM. I exist. Pure knowing.

Being awareness is easy. The essence of being, the feeling of I AM, comes before all experience and takes no trying. Sit. Allow. At a deep level you are being breathed. This feeling of no-breath brings much fruit. Here, you may tap into a deeper region of your being. The heart opens, as a peace beyond all understanding (the mind) arises.

As you come out of time into the timeless you release all worries, there is no conflict here and now, no problems, nothing to figure out or do. You are here, now. Relax out of taking any action. Have no intention. No trying. You are simply here now.

Feel the entire torso as spacious, as pure light, pure awareness. Feel deeper into the heart, lower belly, solar plexus, pelvic area.

There is a peaceful lake of light at the center, the core of your being. The cosmos is within you, at your center. Just as the ocean is in the shell. Don't try to understand this, just relax more deeply. Allow the emptiness. The spaciousness. The silence.

You know what power there is in silence, and it is time now to claim that power as the Christ, as the Buddha, as stillness. Not to rush through your life, but to take time to appreciate every moment; to open the eyes wide and to behold the beauty of a friend, of a tree, of a beloved pet, a flower, of a sunset or a sunrise. To feel the Presence arising in all there is. And to breathe deeply of the treasures you, as the holy Child, have created.

In this time there are many gatherings for the sole purpose of allowing this Presence, this peace and love throughout all creation. Raising Global consciousness is now a reality.

Now we know

Thought cannot formulate the nature of Reality.
Your true Self is already who you are in Reality.
The mind must learn that beyond the moving mind there is
the field/screen of awareness, which does not change.

What I now know fully is that only the Self knows the Self.
That is why as you awaken thoughts are not a problem.
They come and go with ease.
At times there is just the peace.
This stillness is your innate Self.

Being aware of being aware is the first step.
Deepen within.
Find the Source and nature of that awareness.
The Self, the shimmering loving Presence of all that arises,
Is here, within and is here around, everywhere at once.

Grace is here, now.

Breath #9 - The Lakshmi Breath, the cooling Breath

Lakshmi is the Goddess of success in the world and in spiritual knowing. She is also the Goddess of comfort. When the body becomes overheated there may be discomfort. When the weather feels humid and the body feels hot there may be discomfort. This breath is much talked about by Yoga students who also work out. During the summer many have l told me that it cools them down within only a few minutes.

The technique: If you are one of those people who can curl the tongue into a kind of V shape in the mouth do so. If not? No problem. Take a moment to make your home in the breath. Then as though sucking the breath into the mouth through a straw take an inhale. Feel the coolness move over the tongue and mouth. Visualize the breath as coming over the glaciers, coming over ice and snow, cool and fresh. Feel it bring its moonlight coolness into every cell and molecule of the body.

Next: Exhale the heat of the body out through the nose. Truly feel how the in-breath is cool and the out-breath is warm. Practice a few breaths until it all comes together. It may seem strange at first. Realize that you are able to cool the body down or bring great fire through the body; it is your choice. Try this breath when you are heated up and see what happens.

Continue it for at least 7-11 breaths and then sit. Feel. Experience. The inner smile is always welcome here.

Tonglen is a breath of giving and receiving.

Universal law states that giving and receiving is exactly the same thing; it is a flow of energy. We learn to receive equally as we give. The Tonglen breath opens you up to your heart's true sensation, compassion and connectedness.

As you look with kindness on your own sense of frustration, rage, helplessness, suffering or doubt, choose this breath. Your own personal experiences, seen as a bridge to the suffering of others, develops compassion, openness and equanimity.

This is a powerful alchemical exercise which affects all creation. That is how powerful you are. Imagine some aspect of the collective pain, suffering. Now breathe it into your heart and breathe it out transformed as pure white light. Stay in your heart.

The divine love and divine light are here.

Remember: the heart is the place of transformation.
Breathe through the heart chakra
at the base of the sternum.

- Sit in the posture of Presence; either upright or relaxed in a chair. Close your eyes, let the body mind settle. Say a prayer. Loka samasta sukino bhavantu. Or: I sit within the light of the Infinite. I am held, safe and one with this everywhere light.
- I send my love and compassion in this breath throughout the world and to all beings. Namaste.
- Breathe in your own and the world's feelings of heaviness and suffering. Imagine it as a heavy smoke. Take the breath in from every cell all over the body. Remember that the skin breathes. As you breathe this into the heart, feel it change into a luminous clear or white light and alive breath; this you exhale into the world.
- The practice of Tonglen or Giving and Receiving is done to develop our compassion and our ability to be present for our own suffering and the suffering of others.
- This helps to cultivate a gentle and loving kindness towards yourself and others. It helps to break open the armor we have put over the heart. A tender spaciousness arises and the desire that all beings be free of suffering. When you have a loss of loved one, this is a great and benevolent breath; feel the equanimity that follows.

Breathing in Nature

In all things of Nature there is something of the marvelous.
-Aristotle

Being a child in the South I went barefoot with few clothes. Hours were spent digging in the earth with the dragonflies, beetles, earth worms while immersed in the chorus of birds songs. I grew up feeling a part of the forest path thick with magnolia leaves, pine needles and the thrumming buzz and hum of creation.

Now, I realize that I took for granted that everyone felt this closeness and looked for it as I do everyday. While riding or walking in the forests, I knew that I was taking in the radiance of nature. Reading our Naturalists was not the same as being outside.

Now there is an entire body of research for those raised in this modern world of asphalt, skyscrapers, computers and electronics. The Japanese call it, shinrin-yoku or "forest bathing." The Norwegian term friluftslic, translates the Scandinavian reverence for nature and "open air living."

Research data shows that forest bathing lowers your pulse rate, blood pressure and cortisol levels; increases HRV (heart rate variability), and improves your mood. Deep slow breathing in nature takes you out of your everyday routine, as you come into Presence with what is arising.

Breath #11 - Breathing Nature

Forest Bathing and Earthing

"Just like the Earth, your body is mostly water and minerals. Both are good conductors of electrons, and that's what makes you and the Earth electrically conductive..."[56]

Get away from cement and asphalt and find a park or a forest - and it may be a small dell of trees - that you can visit everyday. Walk, sit on the earth, or lay on a mat under a tree. Begin by breathing slowly, inhaling into the belly and torso with a rhythmic but gentle breath. As you walk, inhale on four steps, pause for a few steps and exhale on six to eight steps. Once it feels comfortable, forget the counting and simply feel into this gentle, longer breathing. Let the inner smile spread through your being.

Bring your attention to the spacious sky and the spaces between the trees. Sense that this spacious field allows all creation to be illuminated - all thoughts, all that is seen, felt, heard and smelled. Feel the breath as you feel it expand within and through the skin. Feel the skin to be as clear and light as a bubble. Notice and sense the sensations of the feet, sensations of the colors and smells, and the sounds that emerge near you.

When you are sitting, let the eyes close. As they open, feel that you have been reborn into a new world. Sense and feel with curiosity as to how the world grows around you, newly revealed. Let all of this take time. You are in no hurry. You are here and now and one with this arising. Are you aware? "Yes," you answer. "I am awareness itself." Feel your attention expand as you allow the breath to flow.

Plants and trees also generate phytoncides to protect themselves from pathogens. When we breathe these airborne compounds they boost our immunity to cancer and other diseases by increasing our natural killer (NK) cells. Research from all over the world shows that being in nature benefits our physical, mental and emotional health. Ancient folk traditions from every culture begin with a reverence for nature and the healing power of the earth. 57

Our biggest health problem today, leading to many chronic diseases, is inflammation. The book, "Earthing" shows how being on the earth, barefoot or with deerskin shoes that conduct energy rather than rubber/plastic which insulate, has brought health to untold thousands of people.

Being barefoot, or skin to earth, for a half hour a day leads to:

• A rapid reduction of inflammation.

• A rapid reduction or elimination of chronic pain.

• Dynamic blood flow improvement to better supply the cells and tissues of the body with vital oxygen and nutrition. Reduced stress.

• Increased energy. Accelerated healing from injuries and surgery. 58

318

In honor of the Mystery Tradition.

The Mystery tradition is the spiritual home of many enlightened masters and spiritual traditions. Here is a brief summary.

At the core of all spiritual traditions is the realization that God and Creation are one. That all life emanates from the Infinite One, also called God, Oversoul, pure consciousness. Messengers come to guide humankind toward its highest capacities and greatest adventure; Self-realization, God consciousness and liberation. This truth is part of a rich tradition which existed for at least 4000 years before the time of Jesus.

This enlightened order, comprised of teachers, adepts, masters, sages, avatars of every race and nationality has been the inspiration behind many revolutions in the arts, sciences and humanities. To name a few: the Buddha, Lao Tzu, Zoroaster of Persia, Greek philosophers like Plato, Socrates and Aristotle (father of our western philosophy) Pythagorus (father of mathematics), Herodotus (father of history), Heraclitus, Hippocrates, Euclid and Democritus (father of the atom). Also, Plutarch, Cicero and Thales.

Many enlightened beings, men and women in the ancient world and many of our greatest minds were initiates of these traditions. In more recent history: Leonardo Da Vinci, Botticelli, William Blake, Sir Isaac Newton, Johannes Kepler, Sir Walter Raleigh, John Milton, Daniel Defoe, Victor Hugo, Roger Bacon, Copernicus, William Shakespeare and John Dee. All trained in the great schools of Egypt, Greece, Britain, or Europe. Women there were many. Some were called anonymous.

The mystical Fellowship of Light is known as the keepers of wisdom; they oversee the rise and fall of countless civilizations. In many traditions, the Sun, the Great Central Sun, the most visible manifestation of illumination in our world, became the symbol of the Creator itself, synonymous with the Christed spirit that lies dormant within every human heart.

Mystery Traditions

1-Great Mystery Traditions: Egyptian, Eleusian, Mithric, Rosecrucian.

2-Indian Wisdom: the Vedas.

3-Persian/Indic Wisdom: Islamic,Magi,Sufi, Zoroastrianism, Hinduism, Yoga, Buddhism, Tantra.

4- African Wisdom: Dagara, Djoyle, Bedouin, Dogon.

5- Dragon Wisdom: Confucius, Shinto, Buddhism.

6- Anglo Saxon Wisdom: Nordic, Druid, Celtic,Viking.

7- Island Wisdom: Maori, Kahunas, Aborigine, Cabiri Island.

8.-Turtle Island North: Cheyenne, Lakota/Dakotas, Hopi, Cherokee.

Turtle Island South (Incas, Mayans, Aztec, Olmeact/Toltecs.

9- Essene: Jewish Wisdom, Melchizadek, Cabbalist, Priests of Aaron.

10- Leading to: Cross of Christ Wisdom, Catholic, Calvinist, Mormon, Lutheran, A Course in Miracles, the Way of Mastery

Each path of the tradition leads to the same: a realization of Oneness with the Source of life itself, seeing the Self in all creation and living through the heart. Today this great desire to bring truth to humankind's heart and minds is being reborn.[59] *Desire, intention, allowance and surrender. Let these be your guides. With each breath surrender.*

Be still and know that I AM God.

As always, you are the master of this life. As such, what is arising now and here is all that is. Value time as that which is given to allow us to dive beneath all appearance into what is real.

Dedication

     Sitting on a green and white striped towel in the backyard of this rusty log home, on a hill not far from what is called Cold River, the words end. I muse. The Great River cannot be seen but it helps mold the weathers here: The clouds and fog, the heat, rain and wind always in play. All shape my moods or ignite the horses into a raucous playfulness. She is the Queen of waters. Floating in this bright autumn day, the grasses tickling my bare feet as I stretch them out. The body takes in the suns-fire while the water and wind feed me here. This earth is pure abundance. Her blessings support our dream and our awakening.

     Behind me, a forest of maples, ash and pine trees rise up. Rocks of granite and quartz jut out on all hillsides. The earth is an ode of sky, trees and rock as the swallows, hawks and eagles circle. God's Grace comes in all forms. In the back pasture there is a new being. You might miss him as his spots are camouflaged with the leaves and sun streaks. Look closely as he is keeping watch over the pasture which sits further east, near a small three stall barn. Sir George the brindle mule. He is our guardian and warrior of the pastures.

     He shows us steadfastness.

     At this moment, Candy, the white horse nickers, turns to catch my eye. Something still? What is it, I ask? Ah, the dedication. Many wise teachers come to mind. Many remarkable friends. I salute you all. I dedicate this to you and to the Infinite loving universe. And to Lila, the divine play in the world. I dedicate this book to this field of light and to you, unique, remarkable and mystic friend. Breathe the love and be the light.

Namaste, Elizabeth, New Hampshire, 2019

Acknowledgements

It takes a village to bring a book into the world and I am blessed to have a thriving one. All flaws are mine. My editors and readers have given their time and caring. I feel gratitude for you and your keen insights. Thank you.

David, my rock, companion, chorus, editor and reader.

Jayem, mystic brother and friend.

Karen, sister, reader, editor, friend and cheerleader. Mara and Brooke and children. Vicky, sister in art, life, food for thriving.

James McEnteer, (Mac) editor, writer, father and friend.

Mara Bright, Eric Read, Lark Leonard, thank you for your keen eyes and big hearts. David Shepler, for your artistic and spiritual counsel. Arlene and Annabelle, muses and soul sisters.

Ken Margolis, friend, ecologist and lover of the wildness and the words.

Katherine and Jack, Ames and Jason, Tanyon and Blake Aubrey and Suzanne, Sam, Michaela, Alex, Rachel Zucker, SD and book cover designer, and my Godsons Tei Newman, Sean and Finn Coles.

David's family, Mame, Tita, Barbara, Linda, Buddy and their partners, and their flourishing children and grandchildren. My friends of the heart all know who they are; all those whose lives touch mine and who live in truth and freedom. The Alstead/ Langdon Community, and NH friends- your Presence is a great gift.

2019, Namaste, Elizabeth

Bibliography

Books for reflection

Buhner, Stephen Harrod, All books on Plant Medicine and Plant Listening
Brunton, Paul, *The Short Path to Enlightenment*
Charlton HIlda, *Saints Alive, Hellbent for Heaven*
Dadaji, *Look Within*, edited by Ann Mill, Amida Press,Ojai, Ca., 1987
Dayalu (Ted Zeff), *Searching for God Part I and II,* Shiva Publishing, San Ramon, Ca., 2002
Hallstrom, Lisa Lassell, *Mother of Bliss, Oxford University Press, 1999*
Jayem & Jeshua Ben Joseph, *The Jeshua Letters,* 1990,*The Way of Mastery, 1991,*
The Way of the Servant. Kendra Press, Santa Fe, New Mexico, USA,1994, *The*
Aramaic Jesus (coming soon.) Go to: www.wayofmastery.com
Narubi, *Know Yourself, an explanation of the Oneness of Being,*
Lysebeth, Andre Van, *Pranayam*
McCannon, *Jesus,The Explosive story of the Lost Years and the Ancient Mystery Religions,*
Ralston, Peter, *The Book of Not-Knowing: Exploring the True Nature of Self, Mind,*
and Consciousness, NorthAtlantic Books, Berkley, Ca.
Swami Mangalananda, *OM MA, Anandamayi Ma,* Mudresh Purohit, Omkareshwar, India, 2005
Paramahansa Yogananda, *Autobiography of a Yogi, Self-Realization Fellowship, 1946*
Parsons, Tony, *Invitation to Awaken,* Inner directions Publishing, Carlsbad, Calif, *2004*
St. Germain with Ashamarae, *Blueprint for Oneness*
Tolle, Eckhardt, *The Power of Now, Stillness Speaks*, New World Publishing, Novato, Ca. 1999
The New Testament

Drawings Credits

Cover: Dove Mandala by Channing Penna.
Channing Penna is a self-taught artist who has been impassioned with the
common pencil since very young. After years of portraiture, she
switched over to drawing nature-in-motion such as waves breaking,
animals in action and birds in flight. She lives in Ashland, Oregon.
Cover Design by Rachel Jill Papernick. She lives in Barcelona Spain.

Drawings of animals, symbols, etc.
Credit: From *The Encyclopedia of Tibetan Symbols and Motifs*, by Robert
Beer, ©1999 by Robert *Beer*. Reprinted by arrangement with The
Permissions Company, Inc., on behalf of Shambala Publications, Inc.,
Boston, MA. www.shambhala.com.
Other Credit:
Julia Elliot: Drawings of Turtles, herons, leaves.
E. Bunker: Laughing Gargoyles, Great Grandmother

Websites of interest:

https://wayofmastery.com
Ammachi, www.embracingtheworld.org
Judith@Oakbridge.org
www.Breathingtoheaven.com
Vimeo: the Breaths of Breathtaking on video, Elizabeth Bunker

Abstracts and Studies
Boston study: This study found that virtually all compromised people
(asthma, bronchitis, heart disease, diabetes, cancer, etc.) have
accelerated respiratory patterns. During rapid breathing carbon dioxide
becomes deficient, oxygen delivery to the cells is reduced, breath-holding
time is reduced, and the natural automatic pause is absent in each
breath.

Dr. Mark Sircus (articles)
Effects of Diaphragmatic Breathing on the Heart
Arq Bras Cardiol. 2009 Jun;92(6):423-9, 440-7, 457-63.
Effect of diaphragmatic breathing on heart rate variability in
ischemic heart disease with diabetes.
[Article in English, Multiple languages]
Kulur AB1, Haleagrahara N, Adhikary P, Leganathan PS.

Harvard University, *Now and Zen,* lecture series by researchers on stress,
breathing meditation and other findings, 2016
Herb Benson, the Science behind the relaxation Response
https://www.bensonhenryinstitute.org/research-published-research/

Endnotes

1 the Prophet

2 Lawrence Binyon

3 Thornton Wilder, Our Town

4 Thomas Merton

5 The Koran

6 Researcher Chris Streeter from Boston University

7 John Muir, John of the Mountains

8 The Prophet

9 JBJ Oakbridge

12 Peter Ralston, The Book of Not-Knowing

11 The Gospel of St. Thomas

12 The Way of the Heart

13 Boston Study (Article by Dr. Mark Sircus.)

14 The Boston Study, from research article by Dr. Mark Sircus.

15 Dr. Fred Muenc

16 Rumi

17 Jeshua Ben Joseph

18 Jeshua w Judith at Oakbridge

19 Thomas Carlyle

20 WOM

21 The Way of Mastery

22 The Silence of the Heart, Paul Ferrini

23 Way of Mastery

24 Way of Mastery

25 Jeshua Ben Joseph

26 The Prophet

27 Luther Standing Bear. In the Spirit of Crazy Horse, Peter Matthiessen.

28 Irina Tweedy "The Chasm of Fire"

29 Thanks to Leonard Jacobson

30 Thich Nhat Hanh

31 Paramahansa Yogananda

32 Mahatma Gandhi

33 Amma, From Amma's Heart book

34 The Way of Mastery

35 The Chasm of Fire, Irina Tweedy

36 Jesus, the Lost Years, Tricia McCannon -

37 Readings of John 4:24 from the Aramaic. (KIV: "God is Spirit.") The Hidden Gospel

38 The Way of Mastery, Jayem and Jeshua Ben Josep

39 Jayem

40 Realizing Soul, Paul Brunton

41 Realizing Soul, Paul Brunton

42 Way of Mastery

43 JBJ, The Jeshua Letters

44 Judith, Oakbridge University

45 Sufi master, Irina Tweedy, Daughter of Fire

46 Jayem

47 JBJ and Judith, Oakbridge University

48 Jalal al-Din Muhammad Balkhī

49 Way of Mastery

50 William Blake.

51 Rupert Spira

52 Way of Mastery

53 JBJ Oakbridge

54 Pranayama, Andre Van Lysebeth

55 Andre Van Lysebeth

56Earthing, Clinton Ober, Stephen T. Sinatra, M.D. Martin Zucker

57 The Joy of Forest Breathing, Melanie Choukas-Bradley

58 Earthing, Clinton Ober, Stephen T. Sinatra, M.D. Martin Zucker

59 McCannon, Jesus, The Explosive Story of The 30 Lost Years and the Ancient Mystery Religions.

ZEPHYROS PRESS

© 2019 by Elizabeth Bunker

Dove Mandala by Channing Penna

Printed in the United States of America

ISBN-13: 978-1-5456-6522-0

CPSIA information can be obtained
at www.ICGtesting.com
Printed in the USA
LVHW032239201119
637820LV00009B/1034/P